13 THINGS
Rich People
WON'T
TELL YOU

325+ TRIED AND TRUE SECRETS
TO BUILDING YOUR FORTUNE NO MATTER WHAT YOUR SALARY

JENNIFER MERRITT WITH ROE D'ANGELO

Reader's
Digest

The Reader's Digest Association, Inc.
New York, NY / Montreal

A READER'S DIGEST BOOK

Copyright © 2013 The Reader's Digest Association, Inc.

Illustration © Shutterstock.com.

Library of Congress Cataloging-in-Publication Data
Merritt, Jennifer.
  13 things rich people won't tell you : 325+ tried-and-true secrets to building your fortune by spending and saving smarter / Jennifer Merritt with Roe D'Angelo.
    pages cm
  "A Reader's Digest book."
  ISBN 978-1-62145-102-0 (alk. paper) -- ISBN 978-1-62145-103-7 (epub)
  1. Budgets, Personal. 2. Consumer credit. 3. Consumer education. 4. Finance, Personal. I. Title.
  HG179.M4323 2013
  332.024'01--dc23
                               2013014507

We are committed to both the quality of our products and the service we provide to our customers. We value your comments, so please feel free to contact us.
    The Reader's Digest Association, Inc.
    Adult Trade Publishing
    44 South Broadway
    White Plains, NY 10601

For more Reader's Digest products and information, visit our website:
    www.rd.com (in the United States)
    www.readersdigest.ca (in Canada)

NOTE TO OUR READERS
Reader's Digest publishes the advice of expert authorities in many fields. But the use of a book is not a substitute for legal, accounting, or other professional services. Consult a competent professional for answers to your specific questions.

Printed in the United States of America

1 3 5 7 9 10 8 6 4 2

C2013

CONTENTS

· ·

Introduction

Ah, to be rich. To jet off to a sunny beach in the middle of winter on a whim. To have not just enough, but more than enough, to own that just-right house in that dream neighborhood, send your children to that top-tier college, buy that designer dress or silk tie without thinking twice, and retire without worrying about whether your money will last.

Well, you don't have to be rich to have rich-guy vision. Rich-guy vision isn't just something the wealthy have. You can get it, too. It's the ability to see years down the road and make a financial or lifestyle decision now to set yourself up to get to that goal, be it something you're planning for in five years or fifteen years.

Rich-guy vision means looking at today with an eye to the future. But it doesn't mean denying yourself now to get to that bright future. Instead, that dream trip or designer dress all become part of the plan—the one you will use to save smart, budget wisely, invest in your home and your retirement future, and, yes, afford the little luxuries that make life really sweet.

So, how, exactly, do you get a bit of that rich-guy vision? By knowing what rich guys—and gals—

know about making and sticking with smart money decisions. Those secrets of the rich aren't secret anymore. We spoke to dozens of wealthy people, financial and other advisers to millionaires (and billionaires) and regular people who've adopted rich-guy vision to reach their own financial goals. We had to promise some level of anonymity to dig out some of these inside-the-rich-guy-brain tidbits, but we think you'll find the stories worth the advice.

Once you understand how the rich think, it's easy to see how many—okay, maybe not the ones who were born rich—got that way and stay that way. What's more, you'll see how easy it can be, at any income level, to build your own wealth, to make smart financial decisions and—most importantly—to live a rich life without feeling deprived, whether your annual salary ends in three zeros or six.

Among the eye-opening, money-growing tips we got insiders to reveal:

* How a janitor—and yes, you—can amass $1 million or more.
* When a pricier college might actually be the better one for your budget.
* How the wealthy negotiate the home-buying process in ways you should, too.
* Why you might not need a financial adviser as soon as you think—and exactly when you should entrust your money to one.
* How you can afford to buy a boat or a camper or any other luxury purchase on a budget.

* Why doing your homework will save you money on shopping, groceries and your house—and help you avoid financial catastrophes.
* How saving change all year long can turn into a swing set or a trip to Florida or an entire Christmas paid for in full.

From the basics of saving smart, to budgeting tricks that will leave your checking account fuller than you imagined, to practically-free luxury shopping, to the financial smarts of buying a boat—yes, a boat!—even on a budget, to retiring in style without spending a fortune, we've compiled everything you need to know—the stuff the wealthy already know and keep to themselves. This window into rich-guy vision will set you on your way to joining the millionaires club by fine-tuning the secret financial smarts of the wealthy to work in your own life.

You'll not just become wiser and savvier, but more comfortable navigating your own finances as you make your way to the millionaires club—or at least to that no-worry retirement or dream trip to Fiji. By unlocking the secrets of the wealthy on everything from saving and investing to home renovations and college savings, you'll see that it doesn't take much to adjust your own vision to think rich—and yes, live rich yourself.

Thanks to everyone who shared their secrets, their knowledge, and their own stories of rich-guy vision. Thanks to them, this book will open your eyes to the sort of financial decisions that are much easier than you imagined, and more regular-guy than you might ever have believed.

1

Joining the Millionaires Club

We've all seen the headlines: Self-Made Millionaire Donates $1 Million for Local Library. You're thinking: Of course—he's got $50 million more where that came from. But what about this headline: Janitor Leaves $1 Million to Local School. How does someone with an average income actually have $1 million to begin with?

The truth is, the millionaire and the janitor traveled the same path to get to the mere possibility of such generosity: They saved. They invested. Your bank account balance may be closer to that of an average janitor's than a millionaire mogul's, but to get rich—even a little rich—you have to make smart decisions with the money you have. Because unless you're the next Steve Jobs or Mark Zuckerberg, putting the money you have to good use is one of the biggest secrets to getting rich and living even just a *little* of the good life.

But how? We talked to everyday and not-so-everyday rich folks, and to the experts who helped make them rich, to learn their secrets on what to save for, how much to save, and where to stash cash so that it grows (hint: *not* that bank savings account). Some of the everyday rich folks who agreed to share their advice and stories asked that we use only their first names or nicknames to protect their privacy.

13 Things the Rich Janitor Won't Tell You about Smart Saving

1. You need far less money each month than you think. The average salary of a janitor is about $25,000 a year. Even union-contracted custodians in well-off school districts earn an average of only about $50,000 a year. And yet, plenty of people earning average salaries join the millionaires club.

2. Work more, earn more. When you're in an hourly wage job, there's almost always an opportunity to pick up extra overtime; in hourly or salaried jobs, you can often offer to take on special projects for additional pay. Plus, working more means less time to spend the extra money you're earning.

3. Brand names are just a way to waste money. Does Starbucks really taste better than Folgers? Well, that's something a rich janitor won't be able to tell you. He's never bothered spending $2 on a cup of coffee. And he teaches his daughters that Jordache is just as good as Juicy Couture—at a fraction of the price. Store-brand soups and meats? Dare you to find a big difference other than the cost.

4. A little scrimping goes a long way. In 2004, 102-year-old Montana janitor Genesio Morlacci left $2.3 million to the University of Great Falls, where he'd worked part-time for many years after retiring from the dry-cleaning business in his 50s. After the surprise gift was announced, friends noted that he wore clothes until they really needed to be replaced. He built a basement apartment to rent out and sometimes patched his pants—as long as they stayed presentable. Friends said the post–Depression era thinking—never buy what you don't need (last year's boots just need a trip to the shoemaker) and keeping expenses low (that renter offset household expenses)—was key to amassing his fortune. Of course, you don't need to employ extreme Depression-era thinking or wear threadbare clothes; instead, consider whether you really need a closet's worth of new clothes this season or just a few new items.

5. Covet thy neighbor's house, mirror thy neighbor's debt. Let's face it. He lives in the same neighborhood as you, and you know he doesn't earn a whole heck of a lot more than you do. The truth is, your neighbor is likely to have gone deep into debt to afford those things.

And if not, he's probably spending for the now and not saving for tomorrow. Either way, that's *not* the sort of Joneses anyone really wants to keep up with. Look around and you're likely to see another neighbor who spends carefully and well and has less stuff. Think about him every time your fancy neighbor pops by with his latest (plastic-paid-for-it) treasure.

> **$ TOP SECRET!** Zac Bissonnette, author of *How to Be Richer, Smarter and Better-Looking Than Your Parents,* and Thomas Stanley, co-author of *The Millionaire Next Door,* both discovered that the wealthiest people don't drive luxury cars. "Most drivers of luxury cars aren't rich, and most rich people don't drive luxury cars," Bissonnette wrote. Stanley found the most popular make of car among millionaires to be the Toyota.

6. Perks at work—and what you do with them—matter more than you think. That policy of paying out each year for unused vacation and sick days can be a good reason to use fewer vacation days—think four-day weekends instead of five workdays off—and save the extra cash or use it for the treat you've been looking forward to that's outside the monthly budget. Other things to take advantage of to save on expenses: company car, phone, laptop, and discounts.

7. One part wants, three parts needs. That Montana dry cleaner-turned-janitor didn't hoard all his money. He splurged on occasion, like for a few "want-to" trips to Italy with his wife. But when she shopped for those trips, he cautioned her to buy just one new dress. By focusing three quarters of spending on needs and just one quarter—and sometimes less—on wants, the unassuming janitor never spent much. With $2.3 million to give in the end, the idea is worth a second—and third and fourth—look.

8. Never buy new—except for underwear. Cars lose about 30 percent of their value when you drive them off the lot. But plenty of people are serial new-car buyers or leasers. Better to go for a less-expensive pre-owned car that's only a few years old and has but a few thousand miles on it. Of course, you don't have to go as extreme as retired Army Corps of Engineers civil engineer Waldemar Klasing, who died in 2012 and left more than $1 million to Washington University in St. Louis. Klasing kept his 1939 Buick, won that same year in a contest, until he stopped driving in the late 1990s, when he was about 85 years old.

9. Buy the house, buy the lifestyle. The idea of buying the smallest or cheapest house on the nicest block in town still has merit, but keep in mind that when you buy the house, you also often buy the lifestyle—one that likely includes bigger spending habits. Instead, consider buying or renting a smaller home or one that's in a neighborhood slightly farther from the office. Consider also the middle-ground option of an up-and-coming locale near your dream town. Just be sure it's more "up" than "coming." Either way, your version of the proverbial Joneses recalibrates mighty quickly and you're likely to spend less. It's a comfort to know you could spend more but are socking it away instead.

10. Ditch—or curb—your vices. Start with smoking. At an average of $5 a pack, that three-pack-a-week habit rings up to $780 a year, not to mention the cost of dry-cleaning smoky clothing. And nowadays, many health insurers are tacking on $500 to $1,000 surcharges to cover smokers. Give it up and you've just saved yourself $2,000 a year, easy.

11. You won't spend what you don't see. The clerk and the janitor—and other rich people in regular-guy clothes—have this in common: They direct part of their paycheck automatically to savings. It won't ever hit your bank account balance and you won't have a chance to miss something you never "had" to begin with. Start small—even $5 or $10 a week is more than you saved last week. On a too-tight budget? Every evening, drop all your loose change in a jar. At the end of the month, take the jar to the bank and deposit it into your savings account.

12. If you can't pay cash, you can't afford it. Okay, it's true: Only the already rich can, say, pay for an entire house in cash. But if you ever want to join them, don't buy anything on credit that you can't pay off within a month or two. There are exceptions, of course, but getting stuck in the lather-rinse-repeat cycle of credit card debt and finance charges is a surefire way to stay on the outskirts of the millionaires club.

13. Need a little peer pressure to save for that vacation? Join a social savings club. Like a book club, social savings clubs can serve as a fun sort of peer-pressure way to save for a big-ticket item. These have largely replaced investment clubs, whose popularity waxes and wanes with market swings. Savings-club members contribute a certain amount toward similar individual goals—say, a vacation or home-improvement project—each week or month. But they can be tricky. They require commitment of all members, regular meetings, and a trustworthy soul to both monitor the club's bank account and dole it out in the end.

Great Advice
Millionaire Savings Strategies

Legendary investor Warren Buffett once said, "Someone's sitting in the shade today because someone planted a tree a long time ago."

Think about that for a moment. That big full-bloom tree providing the shade from the summer sun didn't just appear. And neither does money. What unites the ultra-wealthy and the janitor who leaves $1 million to his local school is vision. Want shade 5, 10, or 20 years from now? You have to plant a tree today and take the time to feed and water it from sapling to maturity, watching for and correcting problems.

The same goes for your money. Rich-guy vision is just that—an uncanny ability to see 10 or 20 years down the road and make a decision now to get to that goal.

Rich-guy vision isn't just about the next bling thing—it's about always looking ahead. And yes, okay, some bling along the way. Like that big-screen television or slightly over-the-top anniversary present for your spouse—things you can plan for if you think ahead.

So how, exactly, do you get a bit of that rich-guy vision—at least enough for that early retirement or a dream trip to Fiji—if you aren't a CEO, Internet entrepreneur, or big-bonus investment banker? Read on.

10 Millionaire Savings Strategies You Don't Need Millions to Use

1. Focus your rich-guy vision. Maybe it's to buy a house, to upsize, to own that little cottage by the shore, to take a three-week vacation to Australia, to retire at 55, or to pay for college for your kids. Or all of the above. Figure out which are most important to you—the ones you're REALLY willing to save for—and when you want to reach them: 2 years, 5 years, maybe 15 years.

2. Set your sights and your priorities. Once you've got your list, map it out chronologically. Okay, that anniversary trip is 2 years away and the first kid is going to college in 7 years. And then there's the cottage . . . well, that's probably a good 10 years out. Once you've put your goals on a timeline, be ruthless. If push came to shove and you had to rethink—say, because of a big expense you didn't anticipate—which

> **$ TOP SECRET!** Rich-guy vision means looking at that new television or the next-generation iPad with future eyes and then asking yourself: Do I want this more than I want to retire at 55 or have a 50 percent down payment saved for that cottage at the shore? When you look at it like that—the way a rich guy does—the answer is often pretty clear.

one could go, which could be pushed back, which could be done with less flare (and cash)? Now you've got your dreams of shade. Time to get planting.

3. Stay the course. Now figure out how much you'll need to save to get to each goal. Warren Buffett isn't rich because he's lucky— although, certainly, luck and intuition are helpful. He and others like him started on a path to wealth by having a healthy dose of rich-guy vision. They look into the future at their goals and nurture and nudge their savings and investments along the way to that big day.

4. Save more than you spend. Okay, so rich guys don't always have to do this. After all, they're already rich. But ask them how they got there and they'll tell you that it's simple: They socked away part of their paychecks and bonuses, and they were downright miserly along the way to rich. Consider Betsy, a 60-something widow whose big-earning husband died when she was just 33, leaving her with three small children and not a lot of savings. They'd lived the good life on the Upper East Side of Manhattan. But they didn't save much, something Betsy didn't realize. And the little that there was, well, it went fast.

5. It's never too late to start saving. Betsy went back to work as a real estate agent and immediately decided that she'd always save far more than she'd spend. She gave up most dinners out, pared back her expenses to must-haves—food, shelter, clothing, and some modest entertainment—and a few treats, such as swim lessons for the kids, and two trips to Nordstrom's each year to buy herself new work clothes. Within a decade or so she'd built a successful career and amassed several hundred thousand dollars in savings. The nest egg she grew allowed Betsy to pay for college for all three kids, breathe a little easier, and slowly begin enjoying some of the finer things she'd had before she was widowed.

6. Avoid the lifestyle-creep trap. Betsy and plenty of people on their way to rich say this is the hardest part of joining the millionaires club. Get a big raise at work or a new job that pays 20 percent more than the old one and it's only natural to think about what you might be able to do with that income boost. Maybe add a second week to that summer vacation, or buy a car that's $10,000 more than the one you initially had your eye on. A good rule of thumb: First double the percentage you save, then slide a one-time big treat—say, three extra days at a resort instead of seven, or some new-car accessories on the less-pricey car—into the mix.

7. Little treats add up to a big bill. The big things can be easy to spot as lifestyle creep, but the smaller ones are where the danger lies. You start eyeing the restaurants your boss eats at and daydreaming about the slightly pricier resort; you want to brown-bag it one day a week instead of three or upgrade your jeans-buying from The Gap to True Religion. Well, you're earning more now, right? So you can afford it. That's what Betsy did early on, when her real estate career took off. She started frequenting some of the $100-per-person restaurants she used to, and treated her kids to designer labels. When a big sale fell through, Betsy realized that seven months of lifestyle-creep spending added up to more than half the commission that she would have earned from that sale if it had gone through. The restaurants and fancy clothes went back to their "occasional" status.

8. Don't lose sight of the goal—even if it means saying no. Consider this story from a wealth adviser whose clients typically have at least $10 million to invest: A man in his mid-seventies with millions of dollars in his investment accounts and at least $150,000 on-hand in bank accounts was asked by his granddaughter for a $15,000 gift to help round out a down payment on a house. The man wanted to help. But he said no. He was working on a tricky business deal and moving even $15,000 could have jeopardized it. The deal could mean millions of dollars in profits that would fuel other goals the man had—including establishing a fund to help pay for his great-grandchildren's college educations.

9. Slip-up vs. slip-n-slide. When Betsy started backsliding in her savings and overspending, she could have easily kept doing so. After all, one deal fell through, but she had several more pending. She may have been motivated by fear of ending up with too-little savings—an experience she didn't want to go through again. But Betsy's real secret was in her thinking: A slip is one thing. You can get back up, assess the situation, and keep going. But a slip-n-slide is another thing altogether—then you find yourself going down a slippery, slick hill of spending more than you save and end up, well, wet and worse for the wear.

10. Rich-guy vision recalibration. Even people with rich-guy vision slip up—they invest poorly or spend too much on a bigger boat or more expensive handbag that goes against their own save-more-than-spend rules. But here's the key: Rich-guy vision recalibrates with a few blinks of an eye. Those who make it to the millionaires club may slip up, but they catch themselves quickly before they slide, and they make quick changes to get back on track.

13 Things Rich People Won't Tell You about Banking Smarter

1. Pay yourself automatically and avoid fees. Banks like Bank of America and Wells Fargo will waive the monthly maintenance fees if you have a paycheck or other funds deposited directly. Read the fine print: Some institutions have a minimum direct deposit to escape the up-to-$15 monthly charge. At Wells Fargo, for example, direct deposits below $500 won't get you off the fee hook.

2. Use that plastic—to get cash. At least three major banks—Wells, Chase, and Bank of America—have been experimenting in some states with monthly $3 to $5 fees for the "privilege" of using a debit card for purchases. But ATM withdrawals don't count. Get cash at your bank's ATM—remember, the average fee for withdrawing money at another bank is a whopping $3 per transaction—and use it for purchases instead of the debit card.

3. Cash is your budgeting buddy. Carrying around cash has another big advantage: forced budgeting. You're likely to be more prudent about spending a finite amount of cash than about using a debit to access more than what's in your wallet. Of course, sometimes you'll need to use your debit card to pay for pricey items or for emergencies. But if you're likely to be tempted by that debit card, put a sticky note with the words, "Is this worth the fee?" over your signature to remind yourself of the drip, drip, drip of money that using the card will drain from your account.

4. Work has its privileges. If your company has a deal with a big bank, then you will be as desirable a customer as the guy with $25,000 to deposit. Large companies often cut deals with banks for free checking and, sometimes, slight discounts on loan and credit card interest rates for employees. The banks collect more deposits, and you get freebies.

5. Regular savings plans are for suckers. Most millionaires don't keep their savings—even the rainy-day fund—at the corner bank. Why would they? Even generous interest-bearing savings accounts pay less than 0.02 percent these days. You read that right—not even 2 cents' interest on every $100. Savings accounts attached to your checking account are good for having a little bit of cash on hand, but experts say to limit it to

$500 and put the rest of your extra cash into accounts that earn you more than pennies. More on that later.

6. Bank-offered CDs and most money market accounts are for suckers, too. Certificates of deposit used to be the safe, go-to spot to earn a little interest on a small sum—$1,000 to $5,000—but do not lock up your money for too long. Banks love to offer them because, well, your money is tied up—usually for one to three years—and that means the bank can lend that money out and make more money on interest on those loans. Advisers say that they still sometimes recommend them to rich clients because they are guaranteed to return a little something in a short time frame. Emphasis on the little. CDs pay little more than regular savings accounts—and when interest rates are low, that's around 0.75 percent to 1.5 percent. That's 75 cents for every $100 saved. Bank-offered money market accounts often return even less.

7. My banks really, REALLY like me. Banks make the most profits off accounts that ring up big fees (think overdraft, ATM fees, and checking maintenance charges) and those that always have more than $3,000

> **$ TOP SECRET!** These days, most banks charge anywhere from a few dollars a month to upwards of $15 a month to maintain a checking account if you don't keep a balance above a certain level, typically between $1,000 and $2,500. Tack on other usage fees, like fees for using another bank's ATM machine, and you could end up giving $30 to $50 a month to your bank!

> 💰 TOP SECRET! **The wealthy make banks work for them by NOT leaving their money in a pennies-on-$100 bank savings account. The bulk of their money is in investment accounts that are allocated to everything from stocks to exchange-traded funds and options.**

balances. That's money they can theoretically lend out to make more money. So avoid being the fee-making account and keep a minimum of $3,000 in your account at all times—if you can. And anytime you're tempted to take a nibble at that minimum, remember that the bank will ultimately charge you for it by reinstating those fees you've been dodging.

8. It's not just because we're rich. Okay, it's partly because we're rich. But there's another reason banks like rich clients—they're prime sales targets. Many advisers these days work for a division of a big bank. The largest advisory/brokerage, Merrill Lynch, is owned by Bank of America; Wells Fargo Advisors is owned by, well, you get it. From steering clients into bank products and high-balance bank customers into brokerage accounts or business accounts, the bank can weave the rich into their systems and then offer perks, like discount rates and personal banking services.

9. You can be liked by a bank, too. Make yourself a little more perk-worthy—without the big-dollar accounts—by holding a credit card or mortgage loan alongside your checking account. Chances are, your bank will flash advertisements for low-interest credit cards or discounted mortgage services. Top-tier advisers say to weigh the value of those deals against what you're really getting. If you can get a lower mortgage rate elsewhere and the savings add up to more than the free checking your current bank will give you for the loan, say "Thanks, but no thanks" and go for the better deal—or use the sweetened rate to try to get your current bank to give you the same.

10. Want better perks and rates but don't have big bucks yet? Try a credit union. They have a wide network of fee-free ATMs (often located inside McDonald's restaurants, chain pharmacies, and small grocery stores), lower loan interest rates, and checking accounts that are almost always free if you keep as little as $5 in the account, so you can bank rich without being rich. And just like big banks go out of their way for the wealthy, credit unions are more likely to go out of their way for the little guy by, say, waiting to process checks or debit charges after your deposits are counted that day.

11. You don't have to be rich to use a brokerage-based bank. These days, many brokerages—the place where you can open a low-cost account to own and trade stocks and funds—also own or partner with banks. Partly to drum up bank business—and deposits—the retail brokerages offer some of the best rates and freebies around. Of course, they also hope you'll open investment accounts—an incentive to keep your savings and your everyday cash in one spot. Your account might be Schwab instead of Morgan Stanley, but it's all the same. Chase Bank recently began transforming some of its branches, carving out private client areas meant for customers who have $500,000 or more to invest. Why? They want that money, of course! But retail brokerages, which do most of their business online and cater to a wider range of customers (that means you), have gotten in on the banking business, too.

12. Psst . . . those brokerage banks treat everyone else like the gold-plate banks treat the rich. Charles Schwab & Co. has been a leader among the brokerage-à-la-banks. There are no branches or ATMs, so you won't get your own cozy corner to chat with a private banker, but you will get free checking, interest that's at least five or six times that measly 2 cents per $100, reimbursement of ATM fees, and recently, mobile check deposits via smartphone. Now that's anytime, anywhere, free-stuff rich-guy treatment.

13. While you're at it, bundle that brokerage bank account with an investment account. One perk of an account with a brokerage like Schwab: a free investment account. While transaction fees may still apply, you get the benefit of the brokerage's online learning—on everything from mutual funds to options trading—and there's no hassle in transferring money from your free checking account into the investment account. As for what to do with that investment account, read on.

13 Things Wealth Advisers Know about Investing That You Don't—Yet

1. You don't need a lot of money to open a brokerage account. Brokerage accounts aren't just for the rich. Sure, you won't get the same white-glove service as the rich will at Morgan Stanley or Merrill Lynch, but you can open a brokerage account at Schwab, Fidelity, TD Ameritrade, and other online retail brokerages—with a lot less than the $250,000 to $1 million minimum most big brokerages require. You can start an account at Fidelity with as little as $2,500, and some accounts at TD Ameritrade and other brokerages can be opened with no minimum. That said, some funds and other investments require a minimum—usually $500 or $1,000—to invest. But, depending on the firm, you'll need to rely on the firm's—or your own—research if your account is under $10,000 or $25,000.

$ TOP SECRET! You don't have to gamble at day-trading to tap into the investing secrets of the rich. Investing for the long term is not only more suitable, but also—as proven in study after study—is one of the best ways to build up your wealth.

2. Don't invest in what you don't understand. It's easy to get caught up in a fad, but if you can't easily explain or understand how a company makes money now and will make money in the future, even after looking at an annual report (available at SEC.gov or edgr.com), steer clear. "Investing without research is like playing stud poker and never looking at the cards," Peter Lynch of Fidelity Magellan said more than once. Read a company or fund's prospectuses, quarterly reports (Form 10-Q), and annual reports (Form 10-K) that are filed with the SEC. Look for how money is made and the amount of cash a company has on hand. Is it enough to cover debts and perhaps hand out a dividend or invest in growth?

3. Just because everyone else is doing it doesn't mean that you should, too. Don't invest in what you don't know, just because all your friends have and you feel left out. How you spend and invest your money isn't a popularity contest.

4. Learn the lingo. Millionaires know what the basic investing terms—and many of the complicated ones—mean. Learn them—and how to use them to grow your money—and you could end up like Lawrence Hummel, a custodian for 30 years at a small West Virginia college, who amassed a fortune and left $1 million to the school. Hummel, who invested most of his modest earnings, would sit in on finance-related classes at Bethany College, read up on investing and stocks in *The Wall Street Journal,* and sometimes ask basic investing questions of professors as they left for the day.

5. Plain-vanilla mutual funds and the average 401(k) won't make you rich. The wealthy know that most of the time, fear and greed are the biggest drivers of markets—even if, over the long term, strong stocks hold and even increase their value. Basic mutual funds and the limited options in most employer-offered 401(k)s— like target-date funds, funds that track broad indexes, like the S&P 500, and conservative bond funds—are good, for the most part, for delivering modest returns. Financial advisers who cater to rich clients say that they use these funds to conserve wealth. So use them, but also use other strategies to build your wealth enough to vault you into the millionaires club.

6. Never ignore free retirement savings money. Many employers will match part of your contributions—most common is 50 cents to $1 for every dollar you invest, for up to 6 percent of your salary. That's free money toward your retirement. Who doesn't like free? What's more, the money you contribute is tax-free until you withdraw it in retirement, reducing your taxable income now. If you earn $50,000 per year and save 6 percent of that in a 401(k) that is matched dollar for dollar, that's $6,000 you've saved for retirement by year's end—plus whatever your investments have returned.

60% bonds

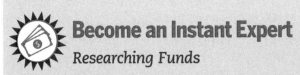

Become an Instant Expert
Researching Funds

For most investors, index funds or inexpensive exchange-traded funds are among the safest and easiest ways to invest. Look for broad-based funds that will give you returns that match or beat their index, including S&P 500 index funds, mid- and small-cap (that's midsize and small companies) funds, and, sparingly, those geared toward emerging markets or commodities. It's also smart to have some of your savings invested in bond funds. Funds that invest in stocks that regularly pay dividends are another good bet for the long haul.

It's easy enough to choose solid funds from a low-cost fund company like Fidelity or Vanguard—which typically have the lowest fees—and either open an account or invest via a Schwab, TD Ameritrade, or E*Trade account. All offer extensive information on their investment offerings, and many funds require as little as $500 to start. The U.S. Securities and Exchange Commission, which regulates financial markets, has a handy guide for consumers: sec.gov/investor/pubs/sec-guide-to-mutual-funds.pdf. And Morningstar.com does extensive ratings of funds and ETFs with easy-to-understand results.

Most financial advisers recommend a mix of investments that's heavier in stocks when you're younger and shifts toward bonds as you near retirement. While bonds offer lower returns on your investment, they are also more stable than stocks—important for making sure you keep that hard-earned money as you near retirement age, when you really need it. A good rule of thumb is an investment mix that's 70 to 80 percent stocks before you're 40, and closer to 60 percent stocks and 40 percent bonds later. Once you're ready to retire, flip the mix to 60 percent bonds.

Before you pick your fund, check both its recent and its 3-, 5-, and 10-year performance. You're investing for retirement, so how the fund has done over the long term is more important than, say, a dip during the financial crisis. Next, look at the cost to invest, which is the annual fee you'll pay to own shares in the fund, based on the size of your investment. A fund that costs a little bit more but has better performance over the long run is often worth those extra pennies. To decide the best deal for you, make a short list and compare long-term returns and costs.

7. Spread the love—and saved dollars—outside your 401(k). The average 401(k) plan offers about 18 different investing options, typically mutual funds. They might not be the best funds out there, and they might be pricier than other options. Funds with sky-high fees result in missed money for you; you can likely do better by investing in similar-performing (but cheaper) ETFs or funds that might not be offered in your plan. And few 401(k)s offer ETFs as an investing option. What's more, you can't use that money (usually) until you retire, so saving for that beach cottage via 401(k) isn't wise. So get your matched dollars, but save the rest in an investment account at a brokerage and keep access to that cash for your goals.

8. Go slowly at first. Start with companies and investments that you can understand without having to study with a professor of finance, and look into ETFs and funds that are highly rated by the investment research firms Morningstar Inc. or Lipper Indexes, which track mutual funds' performance. It's a strategy that advisers say was often key to helping their rich clients stay on track early on—as well as a starting point for many an everyday millionaire. Following a hot tip or trying to invest like someone who can afford to lose money is an easy way to trip on the road to the millionaires club.

9. Study, study, study. Okay, sooo boring. But once you're comfortable with the basic "safe investments" and have the lingo down, you can branch out. One thing about rich-guy vision: It's about always searching for good information—"good" being the operative word. You may not have access to finance professors, but an easy place to start is at the brokerage at which you open an account. Being a customer will give you access to a vast library of information, tutorials, and insight about thousands of funds, ETFs, individual stocks, and other, more complex investing strategies, like options and margin buys. Millionaires may leave that work to paid advisers, but much of the same insight is available to you for free—or close to it.

10. It's a long game—so don't obsess over the headlines or your statements. It's not that the rich don't worry about the negative return glaring at them from their latest brokerage statement, or the headline across the business news channel that sends stocks plummeting. But rich-guy vision means taking it in

√ The **REAL** World

Peter Lynch, the famous and very successful longtime manager of the Fidelity Magellan fund, believed that average investors really could have an edge over big investors. He often said that professional investors didn't get interested in a stock until large institutions and Wall Street analysts recommended it. His advice: Stick to what you know and see; look around for investment ideas in your everyday life. Pay attention to new developments at the workplace, the mall, the auto showrooms, the restaurants, or anywhere a promising new enterprise debuts. After his wife got excited about the fact that Hanes sold its L'eggs pantyhose in grocery stores, Lynch figured that the company was on to something. Hanes's stock rose sixfold while Magellan held it.

patience, smarts

stride. Said one adviser: "You aren't going to become a millionaire overnight. Your rich neighbor knows that patience is almost as important as smarts in growing wealth." Jen, a mother of two from Florida, wouldn't look at her 401(k) statements during the financial crisis in 2008 and 2009 and tried not to listen to the TV pundits as they shouted to sell off investments and put money in cash. Instead, she held fast to her 401(k) and made no changes. In 2010 the S&P closed up a whopping 12.8 percent for the year. Jen's return from slow-and-steady: more than 16 percent, better than the broader market.

11. Don't place all your bets on a single company. It's generally fine to buy shares of your favorite company (we all know people who will never get rid of their Ma' Bell—aka AT&T—shares) or in your own company— as long as you limit the total amount of your single-company holdings to 15 percent of your investments, say advisers. Choose stable companies with a solid history of performance that give out dividends fairly regularly and have at least modest and steady growth prospects.

12. If you can't afford to lose it, then you can't afford to invest it in one stock. Plenty of people became Apple millionaires because they just fell in love with the company and its products and invested when shares were cheap. But don't get caught up in the excitement— plenty of people also invested in Apple when it reached a peak price of over $700, only to see the stock fall hundreds of dollars a few months later.

13. Buy and hold. Seriously. That's just what Grace Groner did. And she left behind a fortune of $7 million when she died in 2012 at the age of 102. Almost every cent was the product of a $180 investment she had made in 1935, the year she took a job as a secretary at Abbott Laboratories and bought three $60 shares in the company (that $180 is equivalent to about $3,000 in 2012 dollars). Every time the stock split, she got more shares. When dividends were issued, she reinvested them. Seventy-seven years later: $7 million. Granted, you aren't going to wait 77 years to cash in on an investment, and many individual stocks might not multiply so grandly. But even after about 40 years, the working years of many Americans, the shares would have been worth millions. Buy solid companies with strong fundamentals—and hold. It's a tried-and-true strategy for the rich, and everyone who wants to be rich.

Great Advice
Know Your Investing Lingo

Investopedia.com, the online dictionary and encyclopedia of the investment world, is a smart place to turn for basics about different types of investments and what, exactly, they do for you. Here are eight you need to know, partially adapted from Investopedia.

Stock: A security that signifies ownership in a corporation and represents a claim on part of its assets and earnings. You can own a share of a publicly traded company like Apple, Amazon, Target, or Exxon-Mobil; its value will usually rise when the company does well—with strong profits, sales, and prospects. You can buy and sell shares via an online brokerage account.

Bond: A fixed-term loan to a corporate or governmental entity that's funded by investors or groups of investors in exchange for a fixed interest rate. The riskier the loan—that is, the entity's creditworthiness and the length of the loan—the higher the interest rate. U.S. government bonds, or Treasuries, are considered among the safest investments but also offer the lowest returns. You typically can't buy bonds outright, but can invest in funds that hold various bonds.

Index: An imaginary portfolio of securities that represent a market or a portion of a market. The Standard & Poor's

500 is one of the world's best-known indexes and is the most commonly used benchmark for the stock market and for many mutual funds.

Mutual Fund: A pool of funds collected from many investors that is then invested in stocks, bonds, and other securities to produce returns and income. Funds range from those made up only of large U.S. company stocks, to those comprising a mix of international company stocks and bonds, and investors are charged a fee—generally 1 to 1.5 percent—based on the size of their investment. A fund's performance is pegged to a benchmark index, like the S&P 500 Index.

Exchange-Traded Fund (ETF): A security that tracks an index, a commodity, or a basket of assets like a mutual fund but trades like a stock on an exchange. ETFs offer a variety of investments, but generally at much lower fees than a mutual fund, and their price can change throughout the day as they are traded. You can often buy just one share of an ETF, while mutual funds have minimum investment requirements.

Expense Ratio/Cost to Invest: What it costs an investment firm to operate a mutual fund or ETF. The most important thing to understand: Those operating expenses are deducted from a fund's assets, reducing investors' returns. So it's important to look for funds that achieve a happy medium of low expense ratios and good short- and long-term performance.

Dividend: A portion of a company's earnings that is distributed to its shareholders, quoted in amounts per share. Most secure and stable companies offer dividends to make up for a steady share price, while high-growth companies rarely do because they reinvest their profits to keep growing. When you reinvest your stocks' dividends, you increase the number of shares you own, which means the possibility of more returns—and better dividend payouts in the future.

> **$ TOP SECRET!** Know the lingo and you hold the same key as the very rich and the everyday millionaire—the key to understanding investing and making money in the markets.

Fundamentals: The information—a business's economics, balance sheet, income statement, management, and cash flow—used to weigh the health and financial valuation of a company, security, or currency and estimate whether it's a worthwhile investment. A company with low debt, strong cash flow, and a healthy market for its products is considered to have strong fundamentals.

Great Advice
When to Call in the Cavalry

Didn't we just say you could do just fine on your own with a low-cost brokerage account and good market study habits? Well, yes, that's true. But even everyday millionaires and the already-rich need guidance sometimes, be it for setting goals, getting better access to advice and investments, or just getting started on a plan. And sometimes it's helpful to have someone who will keep a watchful eye over your decisions and spend the time that you can't monitoring the general direction of your investments.

You can find a fee-only financial planner through their association, NAPFA.org or GarrettPlanningNetwork. com. Fee-only planners charge a percentage of what you invest to manage your money each year, but you get final say on where your money goes. Look for a planner who will charge under 1.5 percent per year. If you need just a financial plan, you can try a certified financial planner, or CFP, through cfp.net, the website of the group that certifies the planners. If you need or want something more full-service, look at a full-fledged financial adviser, either a broker or registered investment adviser. Check AdviceIQ.com for a list of fully vetted advisers in your area, and make sure you go to brokercheck.FINRA.org to verify that a broker's record is clean and their licenses up to date.

In most cases, when you're still on the road to becoming an everyday millionaire or amassing that million-dollar donation to your favorite library, a certified financial planner is all you need. Brokerage advisers often get a big chunk of their take-home pay based on how many things you buy from them, not on the strength of your financial plan.

Just like coveted babysitters and prized pediatricians, hiring a good adviser or financial planner starts with recommendations from your friends. But not just any friends; ask for referrals from people whose general earnings and life situation is close enough to yours that you'd likely need a similar kind of guidance. And a recommendation is just a start: Do your homework and ask questions. If an adviser's performance or promises seem too good to be true, they probably are. Remember, many wealthy people invested with Ponzi schemer and fraudster Bernie Madoff because their other rich friends did.

The already-rich often have financial advisers fighting for their business—and their big bucks to manage and earn money from—but take a tip from the millionaires club: Take care to check out the advisers and their track record with investments, clients, and regulators.

13 Things Rich People Won't Tell You about Financial Advice—and the Professionals Who Offer It

1. A big-bank brokerage adviser might not be right for you. If you have relatively simple goals and less than about $250,000 to invest, some firms won't even take you on—at least not with a dedicated financial adviser to call on. There are advisory firms, like Edward Jones, Raymond James, and Ameriprise, that do cater to those with less to invest—and get paid to do so.

2. Until you make that first million, consider using a financial planner instead. A certified financial planner will help you draw up a plan, suggest investment options, and give you all-around financial guidance

💰 TOP SECRET! To be certain that your adviser will put your interests first, find a member of the National Association of Personal Finance Advisors. They can only accept fees from their clients—you—and not from issuers of any of the financial products they recommend. They also take a pledge to put their clients' interests ahead of their own.

about everything from insurance to college savings and home buying. But they'll charge a flat fee and won't try to sell you products or funds. Brokerage advisers earn commissions based on what you buy from them.

3. Oh, and it might not always be clear when your adviser is working under the best-interest standard. Increasingly, advisers who work for large firms like Merrill Lynch and Morgan Stanley will be "hybrids," which means they're registered as brokers, who can sell all sorts of securities, and as advisers, who take an oath to act in a client's best interest. A fee-based account, where each year you pay a percentage of the assets managed by an adviser, is the biggest indicator that you are getting the best-interest side of your adviser.

4. Unless you've got as much money as I do, your adviser probably isn't personalizing your portfolio or investment strategies. Many advisers use plug-and-play investment programs provided by their companies or a third party—especially for clients on the lower end of the investing spectrum. But that's not necessarily a bad thing; model portfolios can be pretty useful if your financial situation isn't overly complex and your goals are fairly basic, and it's an inexpensive way to invest smartly. It's a one-size-fits-all portfolio for people who are in a similar financial and life situation as you.

5. Your broker's record is clean, but . . . You can check—for free on brokercheck.FINRA.org—to see if a broker has had any disciplinary actions. You should also check state securities regulation databases and state insurance license records. Often, brokers hold several licenses, and the agencies don't have a great history of talking to one another.

6. My goals are in my adviser's sweet spot. Ask to talk to an adviser's clients, and then compare your objectives and goals to theirs. That's important, because if all the clients are getting ready to retire or are putting kids through college—and you're a young couple just getting started—your goals may not be in line with the adviser's primary focus.

7. She's not avoiding your calls; it's just that she's out meeting my friends and prospecting new clients. Advisers survive by building their client base. Most are running a small business—and business owners have to grow their business to keep profits flowing. For advisers, especially those in their first decade or so in the business, prospecting for new clients can take up to 70 percent of their time.

8. He's not really so great with the paperwork. Even though an adviser operates a bit like a small business owner, most don't have the training—or the

√ The **REAL** World

One California adviser, whose clients mostly had $500,000 or more to invest, recalled the all-bust Facebook debut in May 2012. He said that he repeatedly cautioned his clients about the social network's lackluster fundamentals—fewer people than hoped had clicked on ads on the website, and prospects for mobile smartphone apps were uncertain, which was worrisome for future revenue—and what he considered to be an overpriced initial offering. Some clients backed down, but several insisted, ordering hundreds of shares of a stock that barely held on to its $38 offering price on its first day of trading, sinking below $20 within a matter of days. "It's their money. I may think it's crazy, I may tell them it's a terrible idea, but it's their decision," said the adviser.

wherewithal—to sweat the small stuff. Take care to make sure your paperwork, from beneficiary documents to investment plans, is in order at least once a year.

9. He might try to talk you out of wanting to get in on that hot (but not-so-smart) IPO, but won't stop you if you insist. After all, an adviser works *for* you—you have the final say—plus, he doesn't want to lose your business. And as you amass more wealth and become more valuable as a client, it will be harder and harder for him to be firm in his suggestions and advice.

10. You aren't some bigtime adviser's priority—my rich friends and I are. You know that guy you aspire to be? That's me, with $1 million to invest, with friends just like me. That's right, your adviser is paying more attention to me, and everyone else like me, because I have more

money and that makes him more money. When I call, he calls back. When you call, a sales assistant will likely call you back—and probably not right away.

11. He'll probably have an intern or assistant check on your money annually. If you want more than a yearly how-do-you-do and rebalance conversation and you don't have a minimum investment or a magical ability to lead your adviser to big-bucks friends who could be clients, you'll have to pony up for better service. Most advisers have "tiers" of clients, and those closer to the bottom are set-and-forget for most of the year.

12. Part of her compensation is based on getting you to buy and sell more, more, more. Various securities and products have dollar signs attached. Advisers at most brokerages earn commissions on the products they sell, and the amount they earn gets bigger when they sell more. Remember that "in your best interest" thing? Exactly. It applies here, too.

13. Advisers are most valuable to you starting about 10 years before you retire. That's when you'll probably have the most money to invest, so advisers will be most interested in working with you. But that's also when the nitty-gritty money planning for retirement begins—and more targeted investing strategies come into play. And that's also when the advice of a higher-cost professional can be worth paying for as you plan out how all that money you've been saving will carry you through your non-working years.

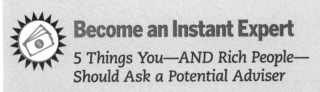

Become an Instant Expert

5 Things You—AND Rich People— Should Ask a Potential Adviser

Investopedia.com offers some sage advice on what to ask a potential financial adviser—before you sign on the dotted line and hand over your cash.

1. What services do you provide?

You need an adviser who will be right for your needs. That may include creating a financial plan and savings goals, tax advice, selecting and managing your investments, budgeting, retirement planning, and insurance advice.

2. What happens after you create a financial plan for me?

Ask how the adviser will maintain, update, and implement the plan, and to see samples of reports and documents you should expect to receive. Lastly, ask how frequently your adviser will be able to meet to review results or update your plan.

3. What do your clients say about you?

Ask the clients how, and how often, the adviser communicates with them, and how long it takes the adviser to respond to them. How often are their goals and objectives reviewed in detail? Have they ever questioned the adviser's honesty or ethics? Does the adviser admit and discuss any mistakes or errors in judgment?

4. What is your track record?

Don't take the adviser's word for it. Ask for documents that prove past performance, both short- and long-term. Find out how often the books are independently audited and who does the audit. And don't be embarrassed to question him. You're entrusting him with your hard-earned money.

5. How are you paid?

This one's critical: You need to know if how he's being paid could conflict with how he invests your money. Advisers can be paid hourly; a flat monthly or yearly fee; as a percentage of investments managed; via commissions on the investments they sell you; or some combination. Ask for the rates, fee structure, and commission schedule, and be wary if commissions are based on the number of products they sell you or the number of trades they make on your behalf.

Who Knew?

8 Reasons to Hire a Financial Adviser

....

1. To guide you on setting realistic goals.

2. For more sophisticated advice or help developing a strategy.

3. To help align your various accounts—401(k), brokerage and checking-linked accounts—so they work better for you.

4. To prepare specific needs that pop up, like planning to care for an elderly parent or for your daughter's graduate degree.

5. To provide a yearly gut-check on the investing and savings plan you've developed on your own.

6. To help keep you on track.

7. To keep a watchful eye over your investments and offer guidance on growing your way to the millionaires club, because you just don't have the time to do it all yourself.

8. For advice on retirement or job changes and what to do next with your money.

5 Blunders Even Rich People Make—and How to Avoid Them

· ·

1. What do you mean my mansion isn't a piggy bank?
It's so tempting to tap that equity in your house to, say, buy a better car or finish the basement—or, in the case of the wealthy, pull out a few hundred thousand dollars to finance a business deal or an extensive renovation. One wealth adviser recalled a client who owned a $2 million home outright and, against the adviser's recommendation, borrowed $1 million against it to fund a business deal. You guessed it: The deal flopped, and he lost several hundred thousand dollars and still had to pay back that mortgage. "He knew it was a mistake within a few months," the adviser says, "but it was already done." The debt was painful to repay, both because there were no proceeds from the failed business venture and because the client had to divert funds from other goals and projects. Worse, his home's value slid along with the rest of the housing market.

Bottom line: It can't be said enough: Your house is not a piggy bank.

2. That deal is set to close next week, so I'll just go ahead and buy that . . . Remember that wealthy businessman who wanted to help his granddaughter buy a house but didn't, in order to conserve cash for a business deal? For every ten people like him, there's one person who will throw up her hands and say, "What the heck. The deal is closing next week; I'll have plenty of cash then." Even millionaires get ahead of themselves sometimes—spending money that's not quite in their pocket because it's, well, almost there.

Bottom line: If you don't have it, don't spend it.

3. Living beyond reality when times are tough. Turns out, it's hard for all of us to ratchet down our lifestyles when times are tight. Take John, the multimillionaire, semi-retired owner of five spectacular homes—three of which required full-time staff to maintain. But when the economy sputtered amid the Great Recession and the man's investment returns plummeted, it took two personal visits from his financial adviser to convince him that if he didn't sell at least one house, his money wouldn't last another 30 years and he'd have to scale back his plans and, perhaps, go back to work full-time.

"It was hard for him to comprehend that he couldn't keep the homes he'd had no trouble maintaining all these years," said the adviser. "But the three [homes] he used the least cost him about $850,000 to maintain every year." After a good, hard look at the numbers, the man sold two of his homes, reaping a small profit on one and saving himself over $550,000 a year in costs.

Bottom line: When your returns, income, or circumstances change, don't wait to act. As soon as things change, take a fresh look at what you're spending and where you can scale back.

4. My best friend knows a guy . . . Two words: Bernie Madoff. Everyone likes to think he knows a guy who can give better-than-expected returns on investment dollars. The list of rich people who lost millions to Madoff and others like him is pages deep. "My friends were all investing with him," said one New York businessman who, like many of his friends and Madoff victims, vacations near Palm Beach, Florida, "and it was like being part of a club to be invited to invest with him." He trusted Madoff with about $1 million. Not only did he lose it all, but later he was taken to court in a bid to have him repay any money he made from the investment.

Healthy-eating writer and self-help guru Geneen Roth had—and lost—nearly 30 years' worth of savings invested with Madoff through a fund that allowed anyone to invest with just $500 to start. She got started, not through some elite investment club or high-powered social circle, but because a friend's dad was an accountant in Madoff's firm way back in the 1960s.

Bottom line: Don't follow the pack. When your friends say they know a guy or that they just got a hot tip on an investment, smile politely, ask a lot of questions, and then go home and do your own research.

5. Everything seems fine and dandy; I'm sure they'll let me know if it isn't. So you read the statements from

your investment accounts every month and take note
if the returns seem unusual—either on the upside or
downside—and make a few calls to your advisers and
portfolio managers. Why worry?

Roth can tell you exactly why. "I paid enough attention
to see that [my account] was doing well, that we weren't
losing money, but that's it," said Roth, noting that it's
essential to focus on your money. "I associated paying
attention to money as similar to being associated with
greed, corruptness, and all that was bad about the world,"
says Roth, who later wrote a book about losing her
money. But now she asks a lot of questions and makes
sure she understands where her money is going and how
it's behaving.

Bottom line: Even if you're working with advisers
you trust, stay alert and ask questions. Getting the
runaround, or answers that are vague and come without
documentation—those are red flags.

Bouncing Back

Lessons in Loss: What Geneen Roth Found after Losing Everything

First came the shocking call in December 2008. Geneen Roth's best friend was on the other end with bad news: Her entire savings had been wiped out. Just like that. Thirty years' of Roth and her husband's savings—about $1 million—gone. The author and speaker, who grew her success from her belief that compulsive eating and perpetual dieting are linked to personal and spiritual issues, spent decades building her self-help business with books, retreats, seminars, and workshops. She taught others to be self-aware, to shake themselves from the fog of life and notice emotional and other triggers that lead to overeating. But, she told *Reader's Digest* in December 2012, once the shock of losing everything began to subside, she realized she, too, had been in a bit of a fog.

"Losing everything really helped me to wake up," said Roth. "It took the shock and devastation of dealing with that to realize I really needed to change things."

One of the first things Roth changed was how she viewed her involvement with her money. She never felt comfortable keeping close track of her investments, something she says stemmed from "old money beliefs." Quickly, Roth says, she realized that minding her money—and asking many, many questions—wasn't unseemly; it was essential. Here are 5 hard-learned lessons:

1. Read A LOT, but make your own decisions. Roth now has her money in several different places, and she and her husband handle most of their investments on their own. She reads everything she can get her hands on, talks to friends, and educates herself on investment and saving options. "But I try to make the decisions for myself," she said.

2. Take responsibility for your own money, always. As Roth told the Canadian newspaper *Globe and Mail* in 2012: "I abdicated my own responsibility for it," because, she claimed, the friend who led them to the Madoff investment was someone who was "smart and savvy, a lawyer and a financial person," so she figured he must know what he was doing. "I didn't question, 'Wow, is this too good to be true?'" She likened it to walking around in a "financial fog." She doubts that she will ever trust her money to investment managers again. Instead, she has taken responsibility for where her money goes and—in turn—for any losses or gains.

3. Ask questions, and then ask some more. That wariness about investment managers extends to how she invests her money, Roth says. She has yet to regain that trust, so she asks a lot of questions, both about the performance of potential investments and also about how and where she wants her money to be. "I have a lot of questions now, like 'What do I care about,' 'What do I believe in,' 'What are my values,' and 'Where do I want to see my money going?'" she said. She uses the answers to help guide her to where, what, and with whom she invests.

4. Pay more attention to what you have than to what you don't have. "My measure of what's enough has really, really shifted," Roth says. "Before, I felt like nothing was ever enough, because I wasn't seeing what I already had; I was just seeing what I didn't have." Now, though, Roth says she pays closer attention to what she already has—similar to the gospel of food that she preaches to people who attend her seminars. For so many people—including herself, pre-Madoff—it's about "the next bite of food or the sweaters and gadgets they don't have and the money they don't have, not the bite of food in their mouth or the sweaters and gadgets and money they do have." Roth says shifting her focus took work, but it's helped her make more peace with her finances.

5. Think differently about how rich you are. Another big change has been how Roth defines wealthy. "I look at different measures of wealth—Am I working at something I love? How are my relationships with people? How am I spending my time?" she says. "These are other measures of wealth. Some have something to do with money and some don't." The payoff is a sort of psychic peace of mind. "I feel like I am much happier," she says, even though she hasn't recouped her losses. "It's a matter of focus."

2

Become a
Budget Master

Living rich doesn't have to be expensive. But getting rich . . . well, it requires a little bit of discipline alongside that rich-guy vision. That's right: a budget.

Wait, don't bury your head in the couch pillows. It sounds like such a downer to talk budgets. But if you want to keep out of debt, manage your finances, and get that payoff—that shade tree, that dream home, that second home, that comfortable retirement—you need to start with a plan for what you spend each month. After all, it's way more depressing to be in debt than to map out a spending budget.

A budget can also help you avoid that horrible feeling of living paycheck to paycheck. Knowing where your money is going can also make you much more aware of how you spend and what you really need. Plus, you're bound to find money leaks—cash you had no idea was just sifting out of your pockets on silly things—and that's money you can use to keep building your way to the millionaires club.

While the very wealthy may not appear to budget—and some don't—self-made millionaires didn't get there by overspending. Remember Warren Buffett? He's a billionaire several times over. But he earns a base salary of about $100,000 a year at his company, Berkshire Hathaway. It's a salary that has not changed in 25 years. He has kept his spending in check and lives below his means on that salary—not on the billions he's made in investments and growing his company. He still lives in a modest home in Omaha, Nebraska. Why? He says the house has everything he needs—he doesn't need anything bigger or fancier, so he stays put and spends less.

If a billionaire can live off what is a modest salary by rich-guy standards, this budgeting thing must have some merit, right? Start by remembering that budgeting isn't some sort of necessary evil—rather, it is your ticket to the financial freedom or little luxuries you're dreaming about. And remember, budgets aren't set in stone. If you make one that isn't realistic or makes you feel so deprived that you want to run out and splurge on something that wipes out all that effort, you can make adjustments. It can take two or three retakes before you come up with a plan you can stick to, but with a little bit of commitment, a household budget can work for anyone at any income level.

13 Things Rich People Won't Tell You about Making and Staying on a Budget

1. Determine your cash flow. First, determine your monthly income. This includes your salary, rental income from property you own, and any other money that comes in on a monthly basis. Next, figure out how much you spend. Keep all bills and receipts you've collected, and write down everything you've paid for in a month, whether by cash or credit card. Be honest and track every single expenditure. Implementing a good budget only works if what you've set up is completely accurate.

2. Classify your expenses. List all your spending under these three categories: fixed expenses, committed expenses, and discretionary expenses. Fixed expenses

$ TOP SECRET! About 84 percent of millionaires say they spend with a middle-class mindset, according to an American Express survey. That means they buy luxury items on sale, hunt for bargains, and more, says *Smart Money* magazine. Affluent households, including those with incomes above $100,000, tend to be heavier coupon users than those with lower incomes, according to a 2009 study by Nielsen and market researcher Inmar. And in a recent survey of shoppers by Nielsen, those same households most frequented mid-priced and bargain stores, like Macy's and Kohl's, when they shopped online.

include housing, insurance, taxes, and car payments—things that don't change from month to month. Divide the sum by 12 to get the monthly cost. Under committed expenses, list utilities, mobile phone charges, food, transportation, payments on credit card balances, school fees, and your kids' allowances—these are things you're committed to. Everything else falls under discretionary expenses: clothing, entertainment, schoolbooks, children's extra-curricular activities, medical bills, etc. As for vacations and gifts, add up how much you spend in a year, divide by 12, and you'll have an idea of how much it costs per month. And don't forget to include a small amount each month to put aside for a rainy day or unexpected expenses.

3. Spend less than you earn. That's something that will make or break not only your budget but also how quickly you join the millionaires club. Take a good, hard look at your expenses. If there's more money going out than coming in, it's time to reduce your spending. Start with discretionary expenses; perhaps eat out once a week instead of twice. Next, look at your committed expenses. Can you take the bus or train instead of a taxi? Can you downgrade your mobile phone plan? Be more energy and water efficient? That can help lower your utility bills.

4. Develop a solid plan. How much should you be spending and, conversely, saving? It depends on whether you're single or married, have children, and how old you are. But a general rule of thumb is, you should be saving at least 10 to 15 percent of your income after tax. Obviously, the more, the better, but that's the minimum goal. Housing is typically your biggest cost and where you should only spend one-third of your take-home pay. That can be difficult in some very pricey markets, but stick as close to that as possible.

5. Get everyone in the house on board. Once you've determined a solid monthly budget, it's time to get serious. Talk it over with your spouse and children—getting their buy-in is critical to sticking with the plan. The key: Make sure they see what's in it for them—that vacation to Disney they've been hoping for, fewer student loans when they go to college, perhaps a little extra here and there for fun excursions, all because everyone stays close to spending limits.

6. Reassess and adjust as needed. Following your budget isn't optional, but adjusting it is. If you find the amount for groceries was just too low, you can and

💰 TOP SECRET! Consider a goal of reaching a 50-30-20 plan, a method suggested by Harvard professor and now senator from Massachusetts, Elizabeth Warren. Your fixed and committed expenses should make up half of your after-tax income, 30 percent is discretionary spending, and the final 20 percent goes to savings. In the beginning you may only be able to save 10 percent of your income, but start with that and work toward 20 percent.

should adjust the budget. Same goes for forgetting to add in that after-school tutor Junior needs to prep for the SATs, or the dry-cleaning bill that is actually much higher than the month you tracked it. The key is to try to stick to an amount you spend—or close to it—even if you need to adjust where that money is spent. If you need to increase your spending to meet your commitments and to not completely ditch the things that you enjoy, take a realistic look at where else you can cut or trim—always keeping in mind the goal of saving at least 10 to 15 percent.

7. **Avoid leaking cash.** Once you've made enough money to, say, obtain that second home or take those two vacations a year, it's easy to lose track of little sums. A rich guy's $75 for an extra dinner out or $50 for a teenage child's must-have mall purchase aren't so different than your $20 impulse buy or $15 late fee. Be mindful of the cash you spend, and if you need to, limit it to whatever you budget to take out of the ATM each week. Cash all gone? Stop spending. If you find yourself needing to go back to the ATM midweek, figure out where your leaks are and plug them up. An extra $20 a week adds up to more than $1,000 a year.

8. Don't overspend for luxury necessities. Let's face it: Ballet lessons, drawing classes, and karate classes aren't necessities, but for most of us, they fall into the category of luxury necessities. They make life rich but aren't must-spends. Check your local YMCA, town recreation department, and other local facilities. Town recreation departments may offer karate or sketching classes for half the price of the local dojo or upscale arts center and use the same-quality instructors. And you're bound to see some of the wealthiest people in town working out at the local YMCA alongside everyone else. Why spend more than you need to? That's rich-guy vision.

9. Don't count on windfalls or hoped-for income. When considering your annual budget and take-home pay, don't include any money you aren't guaranteed to receive. That includes year-end bonuses, tax refunds, and investment returns. Warren Buffett certainly takes home much more than that $100,000 salary, but he doesn't count on it. And financial advisers to the newly rich say it's a hallmark of those who make it up the millionaire club ladder: They live on what they know they will earn and invest and save the rest.

10. Beware of spending creep. When you get a raise, don't adjust your budget right away—unless it's to pay down debt. Instead, consider that extra money a faster path to the millionaires club or your other financial goals. Sock it away in savings. Pretend you didn't get (most) of the raise, and instead allocate at least 80 percent to your IRA or other savings. If your raise is equal to $1,200 a year in take-home pay, you'll feel a $20 increase in your monthly budget, but you'll save $80 more a month—and you'll be closer to your goals. Financial advisers say that newly rich clients often shun the spending creep that can trip you up on the road to riches.

11. Don't be afraid to clip coupons. Academy award-winning actress Hilary Swank surprised millions of television viewers when in 2010 she told daytime talk-show host Kelly Ripa that she clips coupons. She said: "When you open up the paper and you see those coupons, it looks like dollar bills staring you in the face . . . It's how I grew up. Why not?"

12. Remember to buy judiciously. Millionaires pay about $16—including tip—for a haircut at a traditional barbershop, according to the University of Georgia Survey Research Institute. About 50 percent of the millionaires surveyed bought wine that costs around $10. Oil billionaire T. Boone Pickens could own a closet full of designer suits and be able to buy the same ones hundreds of times over. But instead, he told *Kiplinger's* magazine, he only owns about ten suits and buys just three or four new suits—to replace worn ones—every five years.

13. Always shop with a list. Another one of Pickens' tried-and-true shopping and budgeting strategies: Whenever he visits a store, he first makes a list of what he needs and carries only the exact amount of money he plans to spend, he told *Kiplinger's*. It's a habit he picked up from his grandmother. "She'd always tell me, 'Don't ever go anyplace with money in your pocket, looking for something to buy,'" Pickens said.

Great Advice

Modern-Day Old-School Budgeting

Mvelopes.com is an online personal finance service that helps you save and budget through envelope budgeting.

Mvelopes takes its name and concept from Depression-era saving, when families set aside money in envelopes to cover future expenses. Mvelopes allows you to create different digital spending and savings "envelopes" and set a spending limit for each. Rather than monitoring your checking account on the go, you can use the Mvelopes app to see how much you have left in an envelope before shopping for groceries or clothes. By setting a budget that matches your income, you can set aside an envelope for whatever you're saving toward—whether it's a vacation or an emergency cushion—without overspending.

A basic version of the service is free to use on the Web or on your smartphone (there are iOS and Android versions), and you can create up to 25 envelopes. The app utilizes location-finder technology to identify the places you like to spend, and you can snap and save a picture of your receipt so you can remember what you bought. You can sync multiple accounts and create envelopes to set aside funds to pay bills. You can also decide whether funds allocated in each envelope roll over into the next month.

13 Things Rich Budgeters Won't Tell You about Saving a Bundle

1. Seal the house up. Who among us hasn't cringed when tearing open a utility bill? Michelle always felt like her New England home was a bit drafty—and seeing her utility bill in the mailbox made her cringe. She eventually arranged for an energy audit, which cost about $250. The auditor pointed out a half-dozen areas where Michelle's home was losing its energy efficiency, from drafty windows, door jambs, and siding that let in air, to appliances that were energy hogs, even though they weren't that old. Michelle estimates she and her husband spent about $900 fixing the energy drains— and got several hundred dollars back in tax and other state-offered credits. Her utility bill was immediately and consistently $125 a month lower. The changes paid for themselves in less than five months, and the savings have carried forward. And Michelle was able

$ TOP SECRET! Thrift-store shopping trick: Find the day of the week when your local thrift store offers half-price buys, mark it on your calendar, and get there early.

to have her home certified energy efficient. "It was a big selling point when we sold our house, and we plan to do the same in our new house," she said.

2. Consignment stores are your friends. Ever buy a dress, wear it once or twice, and watch it sit in the closet? Or lament how quickly your kids grow out of clothes—well before they're worn out and sometimes before you've even cut off the sales tag? So do a lot of people. But savvy savers get something for that unused dress and lightly worn kid castoffs. Chains like Kid-to-Kid and Once Upon a Child—with dozens of stores around the country—will give you money or store credits (usually with a 20 to 25 percent bonus above what they'd give you in cash) for your kids' castoff clothes, shoes, toys, books, and gear. Second Time Around is a similar chain, handling grown-up clothes, shoes, and accessories. Most consignment stores put your items up for sale and split the proceeds, typically giving you 35 to 50 percent.

3. And so are thrift stores—especially near or in wealthy suburbs. Amy McNenney says she shops regularly at thrift shops like Salvation Army and Goodwill—as well as those run by local churches or nonprofit organizations—that are just outside a few tony suburbs of New York City. She started the practice after her husband lost his job in 2004. With four kids to

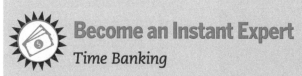

Become an Instant Expert
Time Banking

In dozens of communities, a modern-day system of bartering has become popular: time banking. You join a time-banking group, provide a service to other members, and "bank" that time for that same amount of time's worth of other services. Because there are a variety of people with varied skills or services involved, you could write a press release for a bakery but use that banked time to, say, get an hour of housecleaning or a haircut. Howard County, Maryland, just outside of Baltimore, has had a time-banking system in place for several years. Columbia Community Exchange membership is free, and members offer services from speech therapy and nutritional counseling to errand-running, childcare, dog walking, computer repair, tax planning, massage therapy, and tutoring—just to name a few. To find out more about time banks, go to timebanks.org, check the websites for your town's government or chamber of commerce, or do a quick Google search. Or, you can start your own if your area doesn't have one.

feed and clothe and a dip in their income, McNenney says she looked for any way to save money. Even after her husband found a new job, she kept up her thrifty habits. And why not? "With a little bit of searching," she says, "I find great brands like Gap, Brooks Brothers, Vineyard Vines. All they need is a quick wash or a trip to the dry cleaners," says McNenney, who is also an interior decorator. She often shops these stores for household décor and furniture that can be easily restored.

$ TOP SECRET! When you're at the gas station, inflate your tires properly and check them for uneven wear—both are big gas drainers that will send you to the pump more often. And make sure to empty the trunk—less weight, better mileage.

4. Bundle it—and keep asking for a better offer. You've seen the ads—$99 for unlimited phone, Internet, and high-end cable. It's a bargain compared to the $160 you were paying for the three separately. By now most people have taken advantage of at least one bundle—but it goes beyond home phone and television. You can also bundle car and home insurance or share a cell phone plan with a bundle of talk-and-text minutes (although that might not be a bargain if there's a teenager involved). Ask your insurer and cable provider what kind of deals they can offer. And if you happen into a $99-for-all deal, expect it to expire within 12 to 24 months. When it does, call up your provider and ask for the same deal or say that you'll jump to the competitor.

5. Maximize work perks. The wealthy get all sorts of perks thrown at them. But you, too, can get some rich-guy perks at work. Most large companies offer some level of employee discounts, either on their own or through companies like Working Advantage. In some cases they can be upward of 50 percent off everything from clothing at popular name-brand stores, to 30 percent off restaurants, hotels, and even everyday items and services. Some companies offer points programs, while others offer straight-out discounts, like, say, five-day tickets to Disney World for the price of a three-day ticket, free entrance into museums, discounted memberships to warehouse shopping clubs and gyms, and breaks on movie tickets, cell phone bills, and even groceries. Take a look at what your company has to offer, and if it's something you already pay for, consider the offer a free way to budget easier and squeeze out some cash to add to your savings.

6. Vacation in shoulder seasons. The wealthy avoid the prime weeks of travel—at least to popular spots. They know that school breaks—Christmas, Easter, February break, the end of August just before school starts—are among the priciest times to travel. But the weeks after those popular times can often be half the crowd and nearly half the cost. Shoulder seasons—among them the two weeks after Labor Day, last two weeks of October, the week or so after Easter, and early June—are among the cheapest times to travel to hot vacation spots. Disney resorts often offer reduced-price meal plans and upward of 30 percent off rooms in its hotels in the weeks before and after a school holiday. If your children are younger, take advantage of the option.

7. Hire a professional, and learn how to do it yourself. When thirty-something Nicole was making some repairs and upgrades to a home in Delaware that she planned to sell, she watched instructional videos online to do some things herself. But other things were more complex. Nicole wanted to replace several lighting fixtures but had never attempted electrical work before, so she hired an electrician to install a single fixture. Then she

> ## √ The **REAL** World
> Newlyweds Jan and Kevin saved thousands on a nine-day all-inclusive honeymoon to Mexico by going at the end of October. The couple spent $3,000 on the trip that would have been $4,500 a week later and nearly $6,000 in peak winter season.

followed him like a hawk, noting what tools he used and how he made certain changes. And she asked a lot of questions about what, exactly, he was doing. The visit cost $86. Nicole later installed three more light fixtures and two ceiling fans—which would have cost nearly $200 to install. She saved more than $600.

8. Shop the bodega and ethnic groceries. If you live near an ethnic grocery store, brave the unfamiliar to extend your grocery budget. Nikki, a 36-year-old in Baltimore, lives near three Asian markets but didn't venture into one for years, until a visit from her grandmother, who wanted to stock up on Japanese food staples. "The produce, seafood, and meat selection was varied and of great quality . . . and much cheaper than the local chain grocery store," she said. How much cheaper? Nikki says she spends about 25 percent less on perishables since she switched to shopping at the Asian markets. Luba, a physical therapist in New York, shops at a local Spanish grocery where she says she stretches her grocery dollars for her family of five. She often finds fruits and fresh meats for half the cost of the local grocery store.

9. Barter for what you need. If you, say, are an interior designer who needs a good haircut, you might have a deal in the making. Or if you're a public relations account assistant who dreams about personal training but just can't quite afford it, you, too, might have a bartering deal in the making. It can be hard to drum up the nerve to just go in and ask a personal trainer if he'd consider a few free or reduced-price sessions in exchange for beefing up his public relations materials, or offering a sought-after hairdresser an hour or two of your decorating genius for a full head of highlights and a dazzling cut. But for small-business owners, such barters are often desirable. McNenney, the interior decorator, has bartered for fitness classes, public relations, and other items. She typically gets to know the person or has an idea in hand before she makes the big ask, but she's rarely been turned down.

10. The change jar is your friend. Kathy Reese has had a giant old plastic soda bottle she's used as a change jar since she was young. "I've always tossed my change in it and sometimes single dollars as well," says the mother of two. Her husband started adding his daily pocket change when they married, and her children sometimes add their change. Now "annual spare change adds up to about $1,500 when we empty it at Christmas. We always use it for something fun," Reese said. When she was newly married, she and her husband went to Las Vegas. As they had kids, the money has gone to a family trip, a swing set, or for a special camp experience for the summer.

11. Membership pays dividends on experiences.
The rich often belong to upscale country clubs or
supper clubs that can cost thousands of dollars a
year in membership fees, food, and club services. But
there's a purpose. Those golf games with prospective
business partners are followed by lunch at the club.
There are often camps for the kids and pool privileges.
You might not be in the market for a $10,000-a-year
country club, but memberships have their purpose.
If you frequent zoos, museums, or science centers, it
might be worth it to become a member. You'll save on
entry fees, and there are tax benefits as well—most of
these institutions are nonprofits, and part or all of your
membership is a deductible charitable donation. And
most museums and science centers offer reciprocal
visiting days where you can get into other nearby
attractions for free or less. You may also consider a
seasonal or annual pass to your nearby amusement
park—particularly if you can get an in-state discount
and use your visits in place of other, full-price family
adventures.

12. Points + points + points = a new television. The
wealthy are often offered high-end credit cards where
points are earned for every dollar spent—sometimes
double and triple—for a yearly fee. But these days even
workaday credit cards with no or low annual fees have
gotten in on the points game. Reese, the change-jar
saver, takes advantage of another perk available to
more and more people these days: credit card points.
Reese charges everything—groceries, gas, property

taxes, clothing, and sometimes other bills—on her American Express card, which she pays off monthly. She also linked her business-card account to an airline miles account via American Express. "I've not paid for a flight in five years," says Reese, who uses the points she accumulates from the charges to "buy" flights and vacations. "We've flown to Las Vegas, Florida, Costa Rica, the Bahamas, [and] Cancun, to name a few."

13. Stick to online resale and sale racks. Bethenny Frankel, one of the stars of Bravo TV's *Real Housewives of New York City* and creator of the Skinnygirl cocktails brand, says she never pays full price for clothes or shoes. She's not shy about admitting that fashion is her weakness, but rather than go all out, she told *Kiplinger's,* she is adamant about not buying anything that isn't on sale. She tries not to make impulse purchases, so she avoids temptation and won't just pop into shops. Instead, Frankel said, she tends to shop discount retailers online and frequents sites like eBay for purchases.

Who Knew?

Energy Vampires

Save $100 a year or more by finding and fixing these watt wasters.

Electricity wasters in your home

According to the U.S. Department of Energy, you're paying $100 per year for nothing. The culprits are your "energy vampires," those electrical appliances that continuously draw power even after you've hit the "off" button. Admittedly, some items, like your refrigerator and heating system, need to run 24/7, but many others, like your computer, DVD player, or coffeemaker, don't. Most energy vampires only suck a few watts apiece, but considering that the average home contains 20 of these watt wasters, the cost adds up. By some estimates, energy vampires now make up 11 percent of your utility bill and will cost you even more in the future.

Stop the Drain

Pull the plug. If an appliance has an indicator light or touch screen or feels the least bit warm to the touch, it's using power. You can't unplug everything, but pulling the plug on a few items, such as the coffeemaker, battery chargers, and VCR, can save as much as turning off a light.

Strip stop. Surge protectors enable you to turn off multiple devices with one switch. The Smart Strip is handy when you can't easily reach the strip. This surge protector automatically shuts off peripherals when the main unit, such as your computer or TV, is turned off. The strip has "always on" receptacles for satellite boxes, modems, and wireless routers.

Read the fine print. Manufacturers don't usually include standby power info on the box. A plug-in meter is your best bet, but another way to decrease wasted electricity is by choosing appliances with fewer bells and whistles. Looking for the EnergyStar logo can also help. Starting this year, appliances bearing this stamp must use 50 percent less energy when operating and when in standby mode.

Meter Readers and Watt Watchers

Plug-in meters measure single devices. Simply plug the unit into the wall, then connect the appliance to the meter. P3 International's Kill A Watt EZ will tell you the operating cost of any household appliance per day, week, month, or year. A meter can show you how much money you can save by upgrading older appliances. Replacing a 10-year-old refrigerator with an Energy Star model can save over $100 a year.

Digital meter readers measure whole-house electricity use. They attach to your meter or panel box to provide real-time and average usage/cost information. To find out how much all your energy vampires are costing you, turn off all the lights and unplug the refrigerator, then check the screen.

SOURCE: FamilyHandyman.com.

Great Advice
Secrets to Saving on Groceries

....

Attach a magnet-backed notepad and pen to your refrigerator, and the moment a food item runs out, add it to your list. When you don't keep a list, you're likely to drop into the store for one item here and two items there. Instead, make a weekly grocery appointment for when you have time to focus on your shopping and aren't in a rush. And take your list. Supermarket managers love it when you don't keep a list, because you're more likely to buy items on impulse—and more likely to pay full price for them, since you didn't take the time to look or wait for a sale.

Keep track of what you pay for basic items to get a real sense of a bargain. Buy a small spiral-bound notebook and look through your refrigerator, freezer, and pantry for the 12 products you buy most often. For many, that includes soda, milk, juice, and bread. Give each item its own page, labeled for the item. Take your notebook whenever you shop, and each time you buy the item, jot down the price. Each time you see the item listed in a supermarket circular, note the price in your notebook, too. It won't take long for you to figure out when you should stock up on bargains and when you should wait for a sale.

Although a large supermarket may contain 30,000 items, just being able to find your top 12 items at a discount will save you big money. One frugality expert told *Reader's Digest* that by simply stocking up on chicken breasts only when they're on sale, rather than paying the going price every week, she saves $325 every year.

And consider sharing bulk shopping. Single friends Vivian, Betty, and Nicole share the cost of memberships to warehouse clubs like BJ's, Costco, and Sam's Club. They don't need bulk items, but they all bring lunch or snacks to work and can't resist cheap toilet paper and other items. They shop together and split the 36-roll packs of toilet paper and 48-count packs of snacks. Some of their neighbors with families do the same—or share the cost of a club membership, since most allow the primary member to designate an additional cardholder on their account. Discounts on paper goods, diapers, baby formula, and meats and produce can be significant. Amy, a mom of three in North Carolina, says her annual BJ's membership pays for itself within a few months because of savings on diapers and baby food. When her third child came along, she upgraded to an executive-level membership for another $45 a year, but she earns about $90 a year back in bonuses. Before you join, check the price of membership against your likely use and savings—and go in with that list. It's easy to go in for paper towels, a double-loaf package of bread, and box of diapers and leave with those and five other items you might not need.

SOURCE: *Forbidden Advice,* Reader's Digest Association, Inc., 2007.

Great Advice

Secrets to Saving at the Gas Station

Many people feel powerless as prices climb at the pump and assume driving slower, driving less, or ditching their vehicles for smaller, more fuel-efficient cars is the only answer. If you drive a lot, one smart refueling option might be a gas station credit card. CardHub.com's top three picks for the best gas station credit cards are the Shell Credit Card, which offers a 5-percent rebate on gas purchases at Shell stations; the BP Credit Card, which offers a 5-percent rebate on gas at BP stations; and the ExxonMobil Credit Card, which offers a 15-cents-per-gallon rebate on gas purchases made at ExxonMobil stations.

To add to the savings, sign up to receive your local supermarket's discount card—even small grocery chains often pair up with a gas brand to offer discounts based on how much you spend. For example, Giant and Stop & Shop are teamed up with Shell. For every dollar you spend in the store, you get a point—sometimes items will be advertised with 100-point or 200-point bonuses when you buy more than one. For every 100 points, you earn 10 cents off per gallon at a participating Shell station when you swipe your store discount card.

Wyatt Hundley, a customer of Dillon's, a grocery chain in the Midwest, told his local paper that he regularly takes advantage of his gas points. "I average probably 40 to 50 cents a gallon every time I fill up," he told the Lawrence, Kansas, *Journal-World*. Other chains, like Kroger, Albertson's, Ralph's, Safeway, Price Chopper, Fred Meyer, and Winn-Dixie, offer similar programs with various gas retailers. Of course, just make sure you aren't overspending on milk, bread, and cereal just to save on gas. You might end up spending more.

SOURCE: *Discounts, Deals, and Steals,* Reader's Digest Association, Inc., 2011.

Great Advice

Secrets to Saving on Your Electric Bill

....

Aside from sealing up cracks and making changes recommended by a home-energy audit, there are little things you can do every day to cut down on your energy costs. Here are six easy ways to take your energy budget from eye-popping scary to manageable.

1. Heat food in your toaster oven. It uses up to 50 percent less energy than a full-size oven. Large toaster ovens can fit quite a bit of food, including a 12-inch pizza.

2. Opt for white window shades during warmer weather. Keep them closed during the day to reflect the sun's heat away from your house. If white isn't your thing, add a colorful sheer on the side that faces into the house.

3. Store refrigerated food and beverages in closed containers. Those apples you keep in a bowl on the second shelf and the pitcher of iced tea that's open at the top are making your fridge work too hard. Left uncovered, they release moisture and overburden the appliance's compressor.

4. Choose energy savers when upgrading your computer. Pick from a wide array of Energy Star–

compliant computers, which use 70 percent less electricity than a non-designated model.

5. Position heat-producing appliances carefully. Place lamps and TVs far away from thermostats so the heat given off doesn't cause air-conditioning systems to run longer than they need to.

6. Watch your water heat. Many water heaters are set at 130 degrees or higher. Lower the temperature to 120 degrees and consider washing clothes in cold or warm water instead of hot. Those 10 degrees mean more money in your pocket when the bill comes.

13 Ways You're Wasting Cash

1. Playing the name game. While it's nice to flash that designer purse or suit, other products do not stand up to idea that brand names are better. Many generic household products, including painkillers and cleaners, are identical to their brand-name counterparts. If you insist on brand names for everything, you're wasting cash that could be going toward your rich-guy dreams.

2. Not shopping around for car insurance. An online search and a few phone calls can turn up vastly different rates in the same area. You'll also want to ask about lesser-known breaks. For example, even if your kids are grown and out of the house, they might be able to get a substantial discount if they insure their cars through the company you use.

3. Buying bottled water. Contrary to what most bottled water producers would like you to think, much of what they're bottling came straight from a tap rather than a spring or a well. Using a water filter will give you similar results for a fraction of the price. It's also kinder to the planet—most plastic water bottles end up in landfills rather than at recycling facilities.

4. Paying for free entertainment. Your local library is a great source of free entertainment, from books and magazines to CDs and DVDs. Your tax dollars have already gone to buying these items, so you may as well use them.

5. Ignoring coupons. Stores often place coupons in the newspaper or circulars and magazines you may not see. Ask the cashier if there's a coupon you missed and whether you can have the same discount. Internet coupons can also save you a bundle. Be sure to check search engines like HowToShopForFree.net, FatWallet.com, and CouponDivas.com before you leave the house.

6. Not putting your savings to work. Many people who are deep in debt have some savings stashed in a bank account. While it seems like a good idea on the surface, the numbers just don't add up. Most savings accounts only offer 0.2 percent, but most credit cards are charging up to 18 percent in interest. Keep your emergency fund, but use some of your savings to pay down that debt.

7. Paying for premium gas. You may think that filling your tank with premium gas rather than regular will help your car run better and longer, but according to *Car and Driver*, you'd be wrong. A recent study by the magazine revealed that high-octane gasoline had no effect, except on ultra-high performance vehicles.

8. Playing the lottery. Yes, $10 million probably will make your life wonderful, but almost anything is more likely to happen than you winning the lottery. The chance of winning most big-ticket lottery jackpots is well over 100 million to one, according to Moneyland.

9. Not sharing costs on big-ticket items. Things like lawn mowers, ladders, chainsaws, and other rarely used items can be cost effective when shared with others. Form a neighborhood co-op and you'll reduce both your cost and clutter by at least 50 percent.

10. Needing instant gratification. That new tech toy or fashionable new shoe—think you need them now? Think again. Everything gets marked down eventually.

√ The **REAL** World

First Lady Michelle Obama famously shops at Target and during one morning TV appearance wore a dress from discount fashion store H&M that cost less than $40. Presidential candidate and former private-equity magnet Mitt Romney once told *The New York Times* that he buys golf equipment at Kmart and flies discount airline JetBlue to save money on airfare. In the same article, a friend said that Romney's way of thinking about how he budgets and spends is simple: "Just because you can afford something, doesn't mean you should buy it."

Watch and wait for the discount, and you'll be that much closer to your long-term goals.

11. Getting a tax refund. You may feel giddy knowing you'll get a check from the IRS every spring, but you shouldn't. Getting money back means you're essentially lending money, interest free, to the government for the year. Better to have that cash in your account than lend it to Uncle Sam. If you've been getting big refunds every year (and the average amount, according to the IRS, is $2,400), you can adjust your withholding allowances on your W-4, submit it to your payroll department, and watch your paycheck grow.

12. Throwing food and money out with the trash. The average American family of four tosses out about $2,275 worth of food every year, according to a 2012 study by the National Resources Defense Council. Planning weekly meals, buying from bulk bins in amounts you need, and avoiding impulse buys and marketing gimmicks (like two-for-one deals on items your family doesn't even like) will reduce costs and food waste. You can safely eat most foods past their "sell by" and "use by" dates, which are manufacturer suggestions, aren't federally regulated, and don't indicate safety (except on certain baby foods). Freeze fresh produce and leftovers.

13. Not using health insurance wisely. Don't think you can't save money on health care, because you can. Make the most of your insurance by staying in network. And don't skimp on screenings, immunizations, and other services your plan may provide, like discounted gym memberships and wellness classes. Use generic drugs whenever possible. Ask your doctor if an outpatient procedure can be scheduled at an ambulatory surgical center instead of a hospital. Take advantage of flexible spending accounts, which allow employees to set aside a portion of earnings to pay for qualified medical expenses. The money isn't subject to payroll taxes, but you have to use it in the calendar year, or else you lose it.

Big Tip!

How to Trick Your Mind into Spending Less

One reason it's hard to stick to a budget: our brains. Everything from store aromas, to stress after a long day at work, to a crowded shop can touch off the urge to spend too much. But there are some ways to trick your free-spending mind into conforming to your ladder-to-the-millionaires-club budget.

Think, think, think. Farnoosh Torabi, author of *Psych Yourself Rich*, says it's critical to think through what you're about to buy. That's because our minds are wired a certain way. When you're in a rush or feel pressured, you'll spend more recklessly. Infomercials are designed to take advantage of this brain quirk, she explains. So, first and foremost, give serious thought to your purchase.

Take stock regularly, even if you don't have to. Is your budget fine the way it is? So-called status quo bias means you'll keep paying what you're paying—cable bills, credit cards—unless you have a compelling reason to change. This goes hand in hand with reassessing your budget until you get it just-right comfortable. But, once you do, it still pays to avoid the status quo of spending. Consider whether you can get a better rate on a credit card or pay more toward one next month. Will a rival cable provider give you a better deal? Take stock of what you spend in your budget every three or four months. It's not a budget rethink, but a way to get your brain off auto-pilot and more engaged in the what-if-I-don't-need-this sort of thinking that is part of that rich-guy vision.

Saving money is all relative. Duke behavioral economist Dan Ariely says we're bad at making comparisons: We may readily pay $3,000 to upgrade to leather seats in a new $25,000 car because it's a relatively small percentage of the total price, but we'd think a lot longer about paying $3,000 for a new sofa that we'd sit on every night to watch the latest episode of *American Idol*. Try to think of each purchase as an individual item, a stand-alone cost—be it a $3 food item or a $30 dinner. That is, trick your brain into considering the relativity of each thing you buy to its own value. Then that $3 may seem like a steal . . . or a real waste of money.

Automate everything. Ramit Sethi, who runs the website iwillteachyoutoberich.com, gave some tips on increasing willpower (financial and otherwise) to *The New York Times*' Bucks blog. One key? Pay bills automatically to avoid late fees. If you've set your budget up with a little wiggle room and aren't overspending in some areas, you should have the cash in your account to pay the bills on auto-pilot. That way, you avoid budget-busting $35 fees for paying late, and the money from your paycheck doesn't sit too long in your account, calling, "Spend me, SPEEEENND me" to your easily tricked brain.

Beware of "limited time" offers. Our brains are hardwired to respond to urgency. If you must order in the next 30 minutes to get a deal, it's like a little surge to the brain to do it now, now, NOW! Studies show that when you think you're about to miss out, you will spend, even on stuff you don't need and may not even really want. If you are faced with a time's-running-out offer or a one-day sale, just remember, those offers will come around again—and perhaps just at the moment you really do need whatever that deal is offering.

Do a little bit at a time—often. If you're overwhelmed by choices or feel like it's too hard to spend less, it's easy—and brain-o-matic—to do nothing, says Sethi. "Instead of trying to save a little bit on everything," he says, "focus on your two biggest discretionary expenses," like eating out and drinking, in his case. "Over the next six months, cut each down by 25 to 33 percent."

3

Your House and Home

So you're knee-deep in house research, contemplating which room you'd like the fireplace in and e-mailing photos of homes you love to your spouse, your best friend, your mom. Your dream house is coming into view, and you're ready to call up the agent listed on the For Sale sign. Whoa. Wait a minute. Before you get too comfy imagining yourself lounging in that sprawling great room and cooking in the gourmet kitchen of that home you found online, back up a few steps.

First, get a handle on your financial picture. Speak to a lender to see how much mortgage you may qualify for. "Before you start the search, you have to find your comfort level, get a pre-approval letter, and figure out what you want to pay for your monthly mortgage, taxes, and insurance," says Madison Hildebrand, a real estate agent and star of Bravo's *Million Dollar Listing Los Angeles.*

A mortgage pre-approval is the first step—it represents the most house you can afford and what you might be able to borrow. Yes, the most. Factor in other costs, like insurance, taxes, home maintenance, mortgage insurance if you plan to put down less than 20 percent of the sale price, and added commuting expenses, and go from there. Aim for a mortgage that's about 10 percent less than what a bank is willing to lend you. And if you don't want to impede your climb to the millionaires club, stick to your limit.

Only then should you get back to those dreamy listings—with a side of savvy-buyer insight. Hildebrand recommends sites like Zillow.com, Realtor.com and Trulia.com to get a good sense of your area's real estate picture—from home prices and rough values to information on comparable sales. In some communities, you can get an annual report from a local real estate office listing the number of sales, original and final asking prices, the sale price, and all the particulars of homes that sold in an area—all good to know as you begin your own search.

Next up: Choosing an agent is one of the most important decisions you'll make in the process. There are two types of agents: buyer's agents and seller's agents. Each are paid a commission for the sale, usually around 3 percent. In many cases you can work with more than one buyer's agent—but others will ask you to sign an exclusive agreement, at least for homes you see in their territory. Seller's agents are exclusive from the get-go, for a period of time that's specified in the contract. While wealthy buyers can choose from a select group of high-end agents recommended by their wealthy friends, not-so-rich buyers need to do more due diligence. Don't pick a friend. Or a friend of a friend. Or someone's aunt. "You should [choose] someone who is an expert negotiator, [has] plenty of experience, and a great reputation," recommends Hildebrand. You've got nothing to lose by being picky—the agent gets a commission on the purchase.

When selecting an agent, focus on your needs—someone who is patient, always available, will show you homes at oddball hours, and won't show you homes that don't have your handful of must-haves. Meet with two or three agents before deciding—and don't sign up with an agent until you're sure. This person will be your ultimate guide through the buying process—you need to feel good about the relationship.

Now you've got your budget, your must-have list, and an agent, and you're ready to house-hunt. Be flexible: Remember that if the house is priced right, you might be able to finish the basement or upgrade the kitchen later. Then focus on negotiables, like price, and your secondary wants, like a third bath or a covered porch. "Remember, you can work with your Realtor to get discounts," says Hildebrand. "Let's say you love a house, but the bathroom isn't up to par." Don't just walk away. Instead, ask your agent to try to negotiate a $10,000 credit for updating the bathroom.

13 Things Realtors to the Rich Won't Tell You

1. If I don't like the seller's agent, I might not like the house. Let's face it. There are people you don't like to work with, either. If an agent repeatedly avoids showing you homes listed by the same agent, take it with a grain of salt. You might even get a better deal if other agents likewise resist showing it and the house sits on the market longer.

2. I'm clannish. Real estate agents are a tight-knit group, especially those in small towns, gated communities, or tony enclaves, and are more comfortable working with people they know. An agent is likely to steer you away from homes listed by out-of-town brokers—you'll have to specifically ask to see them. They're wary of getting involved in a business deal with an unknown quantity, but sometimes a little risk nets a big reward when that out-of-towner's listing doesn't move fast and the "price reduced" sign comes out.

3. An open house is all about me. The majority of visitors are nosy neighbors and people just starting their house-hunt—so the listing agent has an opportunity to gain new clients. If you don't have an agent yet, give as little info as possible on the open house sign-in sheet, lest you suffer through weeks of sales calls pitching the open house agent's services. And if you do have an agent, ask them to show you the property either before or after the open house.

4. If I'm hugely successful, you may not get the benefit of my experience. A well-known agent may pass you off to a junior agent after you sign the contract—especially if you're looking at lower-priced homes. Agents are businesspeople, after all, and the bigger the price, the bigger their paycheck. And before signing a contract for either a buyer's or a seller's agent, make sure you get your money's worth, and find out exactly who will be handling your calls, showing you homes, and, if you're selling, marketing your property.

5. Read the fine print. A contract may include an extra "administrative fee" of $250 to $1,500 on top of the agent's commission to cover the brokerage office's costs. But the fee is negotiable—and the commission can be, too. Most agents charge 3 percent, but if both your agent and the seller's agent for the house you're buying work at the same brokerage, you may be able to shave off a percentage point or even two, so you'll pay a 4 or 5 percent commission instead of the standard 6 percent. Some agents may also knock a percentage point off their commission to get a deal done. Just ask.

6. Beauty—and value—is in the eye of the beholder. Even at the high end of the real estate market, lux touches like marble countertops, double bathroom sinks, bonus rooms, and higher-end finishes can add thousands— or hundreds of thousands— to a home's value. Even a very similar home that's got a better view, a choicer lot, or a lusher landscape can fetch more. "A pool is a 'must-have' for some and a 'no way I'm taking care of that' for others," says Ryan Serhant, a New York City real estate agent who stars on Bravo television's *Million Dollar Listing New York*. "Value only exists for a person that sees value."

7. Don't believe everything you read online— especially not property values. Sites like Zillow.com assess how nearby homes with similar square footage have sold and local tax assessor rolls will show how a town values a home. Both can be misleading, outdated, or brought out of whack by, say, a foreclosure or a fixer-upper that sold for half the value of its neighbors. Trust your agent's knowledge of the neighborhood and the homes in your price point, even if it makes you cringe.

$ **TOP SECRET!** Buyers at any price point need an expert to guide them through finding, assessing, and buying the right home, especially the first time around. So before you hire an agent, consider their expertise and insight and how real estate purchases get done in your target town. Find someone who will be knowledgeable and confident enough to clue you in throughout the process as an advocate, not just a yes-agent.

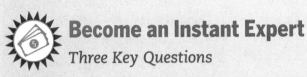

Become an Instant Expert
Three Key Questions

Madison Hildebrand, real estate agent and star of Bravo's *Million Dollar Listing Los Angeles*, says every would-be buyer should ask themselves these key questions before deciding on your must-haves:

What's my goal? Is this a long-term move and investment? Is it a starter home that you'll either sell or rent out later? Keep that in mind.

What's the right loan for me? "You should be more aggressive about finding the right loan if it's a long-term investment, because it will save you money," advises Hildebrand. "You're going to make that money up because your payments will be so much lower." If you expect to move within five years, think about an adjustable-rate loan—but beware that there are big risks as interest rates rise. In 2012 many people who otherwise would've considered an adjustable mortgage instead took 30-year fixed loans and locked in historically low rates—some as low as 3.25 percent. And consider a 15-year mortgage, where rates can be more than a full percentage point lower than a 30-year loan.

What details are important to me? Do you want to be in the right school system, next to a park, or is light the most important thing? "If you live in a hot state," says Hildebrand, "you're gonna want to face north." Other things to consider: walking distance to restaurants or transportation, the size of a garage, laundry room location, entry closets, and other particulars that aren't easily changeable.

8. About that finished basement and enclosed sun porch . . . They're great, right? Too bad they aren't up to code or permitted properly. Even the wealthy get stuck with renovation nightmares. For the rich, getting a property up to code might mean pocket change, but for most people it can be costly—especially if the building inspector makes you tear it down and start over.

9. The customer isn't always right. You need an agent who is willing to tell it like it is—to be honest with you about the value of a home, the type of loan you're considering, the problems or challenges she sees. That's not always the case with agents, who make money only when you make a purchase. "If I believe a client is making a mistake, I will tell him so," said Dolly Lenz, real estate agent to the rich and famous and vice chairman at Prudential Douglas Elliman, to CNBC in late 2012. The very wealthy are used to being in charge, handling big deals at the office, and demanding top-notch service and quick results. But the reason the mega-rich hire a real estate agent is because they need a certain expertise that they don't have.

10. I'll try to push up your price limit. Even the wealthy have price limits. But that doesn't mean their real estate agents—or yours—won't show homes that might be 10 percent or more above that tippy-top limit. In some cases the agent may know the home is overpriced. But remember, he or she is working off a commission. So that price bump is lining their pocket with money that you hadn't planned to spend. Stick to your comfort level.

11. And I won't stop you from paying too much. In Realtor parlance a house is worth whatever the buyer is willing to pay—even if the agent is secretly snickering over your too-high offer. Melissa and Thomas got the sinking feeling that they overpaid after their neighbors' larger homes went on the market for only $20,000 more than they'd paid. Melissa thought nothing of it when her agent told her that the house was worth what she felt it was worth. Paying 5 percent more on a house that should be valued at $200,000 means paying tens of thousands more in interest and mortgage payments over 30 years. Or that you won't recover the costs of any improvements when you sell. Insist that your agent be frank about the home's value—even if it means walking away when the seller won't budge.

12. My rich clients demand confidentiality. It's no surprise that wealthy buyers insist that agents keep mum, considering their real estate transactions can be well into the millions. But every buyer should demand confidentiality. Once you settle into a new town, you don't want to find out that the agent blabbed about your credit or how picky you were to another agent who turns out to be your neighbor or the parent of your child's new best friend.

√ The **REAL** World

A buyer in a tony New York City suburb almost bought into a construction nightmare. Katherine and her husband fell in love with a two-floor bungalow that had a basement refinished to include a third bathroom, a bedroom, and a playroom. As they were about to make an offer, they went back for another look and noticed some wiring slightly askew and some finishes that seemed . . . well, not quite finished. It turned out that the work was done without permits—or inspection. The town's inspector was notorious for making new owners tear out work—even if it was up to code. Katherine and her husband walked away.

13. PLEASE use my inspector. Most buyer's last step before signing a contract is to pay between $400 and $1,000 (for a high-end home) for a home inspection to spot potentially pricey problems—and then cite them to either bargain down the price or walk away. Ignore your agent's recommendations; they're likely to be for inspectors who make the process smoother. Do the legwork and scour online reviews for the most meticulous professionals. Otherwise, you could find yourself replacing $50,000 worth of plumbing that a gloss-over inspector deemed was just fine.

Bouncing Back

When the Dream House Is a Nightmare

....

Anna L. and her husband had their hearts set on a three-bedroom, two-bath bungalow with a tidy backyard and full basement that was big enough to be turned into a rec room or playroom. Their real estate agent pushed them to make an offer—quick; the price was right, and the yard and basement were bigger than comparable houses in the Queens, New York, neighborhood.

The couple—secretly expecting their first child at the time—was smitten. They'd already imagined their nursery just next door to the light-filled master bedroom on the second floor. They'd even measured the backyard to figure out what size swing set might fit and taken measurements and photos of a covered porch in hopes of having a contractor friend ballpark a price to turn it into another room. In their minds, Anna and her husband already lived in the brick house. Then they noticed what looked like a few cracks in the foundation, and Anna's father, who came by to see the house just before the couple was set to make an offer, smelled something odd in the basement and suspected mold.

"I started to get a little nervous, but our agent was insisting we make the offer because other offers were coming in on the house," says Anna. "So we did."

The offer was accepted the next day, and the seller pushed to go to contract within the next few days. Anna fended off the anxious owner, and at the same time, her husband arranged for an engineer and a home inspector to come to the house—on the double. Anna hoped the smell and the cracks were no big deal, but meanwhile, she'd noticed some hidden panels in the basement and patched-up spots hidden behind furniture in the living room. What were they for? Why were they there?

Two words: money pit. The engineer found deep cracks in the foundation. The house would need extensive repairs—to the tune of tens of thousands of dollars. The home inspector had worse news. That smell, those patched-up spots? It was mold. The sellers had apparently tried to remedy the problem themselves, pulling open small portions of dry wall and then patching them back up. But the mold in the basement behind the partly sheetrocked walls was extensive and spreading up the walls inside the house. What's more, the plumbing was ancient and corroded and would need to be replaced completely. Together the mold remediation and the plumbing work alone could cost $40,000 or more. There were a dozen other items checked off on the inspection report for remediation within 12 to 18 months.

Anna and her husband were devastated. But, she says, after a weekend lamenting the loss of their dream-house-turned-nightmare, they were circumspect about the situation. "Thank God we didn't follow the Realtor's advice and just go for it. The house was just one big money pit," she said.

You can't avoid some of the usual maintenance items—gutters that pull away from the house and need to be replaced, old wooden supports that need to be reinforced on older homes, for instance—but you can avoid buying a home that will drain your savings. Never let yourself be rushed into an offer or a contract, and always spend the extra money on a home inspection and—if you have structural concerns or are buying an older home—an engineer to do a thorough assessment and give you a clear picture of what you're in for.

Who Knew?
Home Buying 101—The Basics

Okay, you've picked your town, your agent, and have saved enough for a down payment. And YES! You've found your dream home at what you consider a fair price. Now what? Read on.

The offer. This is what you believe to be a fair price for the house you want. Unless there are a lot of other potential buyers and you expect the bidding to be competitive, it's best not to offer your absolute maximum—in most cases, offer 10 to 20 percent below the asking price. Your agent will make the offer to the seller's agent, and then the negotiations begin. The seller may come back with a counteroffer, and you may in turn make a new offer. A seller's counteroffer for a higher price may include an offer to, say, pay part of the closing costs or give a credit toward the costs of repairs or work.

The home inspection. Once you've agreed upon a price, it's important to make sure you know what you're getting into. Hire a picky—and licensed—home inspector, no matter how new the home is or how great it looks. An inspector will evaluate the home's structure; construction; heating, cooling, plumbing, and electrical systems; and identify what needs to be repaired or replaced. They'll also give you a sense of how quickly work needs to be done. Walk through the inspection with your hired pro. Expect to pay between about $300 and $800, depending on location, size of the home, and extra tests you might want, like lead paint testing. Within a few days you'll receive a detailed report. Better to find out BEFORE you've plunked down your cash that your sewer line needs to be replaced ASAP than after you've moved your furniture in. This way, you can renegotiate the price.

The contract. Your real estate agent or, in some states, real estate attorney, will draw up a contract with the sale price and proposed closing date. It should also detail circumstances that allow you to back out without losing your deposit or down payment. Among them: if you can't secure a mortgage within a specified period —usually 30 to 45 days—or if the appraisal comes in far below the offer price and jeopardizes the mortgage. Remember: Once you sign the contract, backing out for any other reason usually means you'll lose your deposit.

The appraisal. Yet another good reason to get an agent who really knows the market you're buying in: Your lender will have the house appraised to assess its fair market value, based on comparable sales, the home's condition, upgrades, and the like. (You'll foot the $400 to $800 bill—and it's not refundable.) The appraisal should come in within a few thousand dollars of your offer. But if it's far below your offer, you may not be able to borrow as much and will either have to pony up extra cash, negotiate the price down—or walk away.

The down payment. This a percentage of the purchase price that you'll have to pay in cash. Many first-time buyers with little cash on hand take advantage of Federal Housing Administration (FHA)–backed mortgages, which allow you to put down just under 5 percent. But you'll pay steep mortgage insurance fees—about $3,600 upfront and $300 a month on a $300,000 loan with 5 percent down— for at least the first five years of the loan. If you've got a down payment of more than 10 percent, you can qualify for a traditional loan with a lower insurance premium. Want to avoid the fee altogether? Put down 20 percent.

The mortgage. The most common is a 30-year fixed-rate loan, with steady payments over the term. There are also 15-year fixed rate loans and adjustable-rate mortgages, or ARMs, which offer low interest for three to seven years, after which the rate is reset every year. But unless you have a crystal ball, ARMs aren't a good idea for most people because rates could rocket up 5 or 6 percentage points after that initial honeymoon period. Be prepared to provide a lot of paperwork: tax returns, pay stubs, bank and retirement account statements, proof of employment, a credit check, and much more.

Your property taxes. Your tax dollars will pay for garbage pickup, schools, the town parks, and pool, so get a realistic assessment of the total cost and figure it into your monthly expenses. Your mortgage lender may want to escrow taxes—that is, collect them every month with your mortgage payment. If not, it'll be up to you to save that money and pay the local tax assessor on time.

Great Advice

The Mortgage That Isn't Right for Most

It's an understandable temptation: Your own research on mortgages turns up—or your mortgage broker mentions—an interest-only loan to buy your new home. The attraction is clear, what with lower payments of just the interest—often saving several hundred dollars a month on a $300,000 mortgage—and later a loan reset that means bigger payments but usually a still-relatively low interest rate. After all, you expect your home to rise in value, and your income is bound to go up since you're on the management track.

According to Investopedia, "interest-only mortgages can be useful for first-time home buyers because it allows young people to defer large payments until their incomes grow." Once the interest-only term ends (usually after 5 or 10 years), borrowers can get another, shorter interest-only term or move into a conventional 30-year mortgage—with payments that will be several hundred dollars more than the interest-only payments.

Sounds great, right? Not exactly. There are some major pitfalls of interest-only. First, you build absolutely no equity in your home since you aren't paying down the principal. And second, if your home loses value, you are underwater on your loan almost immediately—in other words, you owe more on the mortgage than the house is worth.

Just ask Kristine and John. They bought a house near the end of the run-up of home prices, in 2006. They took a "great" deal—an interest-only 10-year loan—figuring their home's value would go up, they'd be earning more, and, anyway, they'd likely sell their house and trade up before the 10-year period ended. Fast-forward a few years to a housing collapse, home price declines, and, for Kristine and John, a severely underwater mortgage on a home that they'd even put 20 percent down on. When a job transfer came along, John went—without the family—for a year, commuting back and forth on weekends because the couple couldn't sell their house. Its value had shrunk 30 percent, and they had no equity. They owed more than the house was worth, and no lender would allow them to refinance.

For three years the couple made extra payments toward the principal, and finally, with the real estate market recovering and home prices increasing, they owe exactly what their home is worth. Even so, no lender will offer them refinancing—since they're technically mortgaged at 100 percent of their home's appraised value. They say they'll keep paying extra toward the principal on the loan until they can refinance—every extra cent in their budget goes to that purpose. Plans they had for improving the house are on hold indefinitely, since they'd just be underwater again if they spent to make them.

Meanwhile, Kristine passed up a lucrative job a few states away, and John transferred so he could live at home again, delaying a promotion that he'd anticipated.

"It seemed like such a great idea at the time, when the market was only going up, up, up," says Kristine. "I never thought we'd be stuck here."

13 Things Your Mortgage Lender Won't Tell You

1. You can get a better deal if you don't go directly to the bank. Mortgage brokers and originators almost always offer lower interest rates than a big bank. If you start with your bank branch, you could end up with a rate that's 1 percentage point or more higher—even if you have great credit and a decent down payment. Ask around for a reputable broker. Your real estate agent likely has a list of several with whom their clients have worked—in this case, these are good recommendations to have.

2. Get pre-approved by a mainstream bank or credit union. In some places a Realtor won't even take you to see properties unless you have a pre-approval letter and likely loan amount. Mortgage brokers also use that pre-approval figure as a loan limit. Banks' stringent lending requirements give a bank pre-approval real clout. The paperwork isn't as onerous as that for your mortgage; it includes bank statements, proof of income, and info on investment accounts and savings, plus a credit check. But once you've found the home you want to buy, you can shop around for other lenders, better terms, or a lower rate.

3. Low fees often come with a cost—usually higher interest rates. Paying a low fee now for the standard mortgage costs—for originating, closing, and servicing the loan—could mean being stuck with a higher interest rate for 30 years. On a $300,000 mortgage, a difference of even one-quarter percent could mean paying tens of thousands more in interest over time. Ask your lender if you can pay a higher fee upfront to get a lower rate. It can save you far more than the extra $1,000 you fork over at closing.

4. It'll cost you if it takes longer than 60 days to close. That super-low rate you locked in may expire after 60 days and you'll have to pay a fee to keep it—anywhere from $250 to $750. If mortgage rates are on the way up, you'll want to pay it to save thousands in interest. But it sure can sting just as you're about to part with a big chunk of change to buy a home in the first place.

5. If rates drop, I can reduce yours—if you remind me. Mortgage rates, set by the cost of 10-year Treasury notes, can vary from week to week and even day to day. But what your mortgage lender probably won't tell you is that if they drop when you're zeroing in on your closing date, you can float your rate down to the new, lower rate. Ask.

6. Virtual lenders, like LendingTree.com and Quicken Loans, really can save you money, but I'll pan them. Online-only lenders siphon customers—and fees— away from banks and brokers. So a bricks-and-mortar lender may try to scare you into worrying about hidden fees, closing snafus, and the like. But you can get a great rate from a virtual lender—and some mortgage pros admit that these lenders face more scrutiny simply because they are web-based.

7. Just say no to fees. Don't agree to any prepayment penalties or extra servicing fees, which are more common with online lenders. Negotiate them away.

8. You can still use your credit cards while your mortgage is being underwritten. But avoid big purchases, overcharging, and anything out of the ordinary. Mortgage underwriters look at each card to see how much of your available credit you use—try to keep it under 30 percent. And no matter how great a credit card transfer offer might be, just say no until after your mortgage is approved. Transferring debt opens a credit inquiry, and that could harm your credit score.

9. If your taxes are being escrowed, we'll either take too much or not enough. Plain and simple, lenders use outdated information to estimate your tax obligations—especially if you buy during the summer, when towns generally revise their property-tax assessments. Sit down with the local tax assessor and

get a clear picture of what you might owe. If your lender doesn't take enough or taxes go up—and they usually do—they'll make an adjustment and send you a bill for the difference. Be prepared: It may be several hundred dollars. You can spread the amount out over the next year's mortgage payments, but if you can, pay upfront and keep your payments lower.

10. That low-money-down FHA loan has an expensive catch. With an FHA mortgage, your down payment is about 5 percent of the home's sale price. But not only will you pay hefty monthly mortgage-insurance premiums, you'll pay them for at least five years—even if you refinance or pay down the loan principle early to less than 80 percent of the home's value.

11. It's okay to use gifted cash to help reach that down payment. About 25 percent of first-time home buyers use gifts from relatives to help bolster a down payment, according to data from the National Association of Realtors. But lenders want to make very certain that the money you get is a gift and not a loan. Ask the giver to give you a letter that verifies their relationship, the amount given, and wording that specifies that the money is a gift, not to be repaid. Even better, have the money deposited in your bank account at least four months before you apply for a mortgage—lenders usually only look at three prior month's of statements. If a few thousand dollars will make the difference between private mortgage insurance or that FHA loan catch, it may be worth the careful planning.

12. About those closing costs . . . In some states closing costs can top $10,000. In others they average closer to $3,000—with fees for recording the deed, the bank's closing costs, title insurance, taxes due within 30 days, and more rolled into what you'll need to bring to the table. Why the wide range? In some states it's unheard of to go to closing without an attorney—rather, three: one for the buyer, one for the seller, and one for the lender. Plus, title insurance has gotten pricier. Shop around for services like title insurance (in most states) or a closing attorney.

13. Paying points to get a lower interest rate is worth it—sometimes. A discount point is an upfront payment of 1 percent of the loan amount, paid at closing, in exchange for a reduction in the interest rate—as a rule of thumb, a quarter-percentage point for each discount point you pay. You end up with a lower monthly mortgage payment by virtue of a lower interest rate. If you plan to stay in your home and keep the first mortgage for at least five years, it can be worth it to pay upfront points—one point on a $200,000 mortgage will cost you $2000 at closing—although the value of that lower rate really kicks in closer to the 10-year mark, when the interest savings can reach tens of thousands of dollars.

Who Knew?
Consider a Two-Family Home

....

Remember that rich-guy vision of finding a way to make money off your home? For many people the answer is a two-family house.

You may take on a bigger mortgage, but the rental income from the second residence—be it a one-bedroom apartment or a full-floor family home—can offset the costs and help you build equity faster. AnneMarie and Joseph, a couple with two small children who left the bustle of New York City for a quaint suburb nearby, were able to afford a slightly larger home with a more convenient commute by buying a two-family home. They occupy the first floor and basement—three bedrooms, two baths, kitchen, and living, dining, and family rooms—and the rent on the two-bedroom, one-bath apartment on the second floor cuts their mortgage payments by just over a third.

The trade-off is that you are now a landlord. AnneMarie and Joseph said that took some getting used to, from screening tenants' credit-worthiness to the rental's repairs and maintenance. They took classes at Home Depot, read DIY books and online articles, shopped scratch-and-dent sales for appliances, and hired out for the big stuff, like plumbing. Then, after some upgrades, they were able to rent the apartment out for 20 percent more than they had before. The couple plans to either sell and move to a larger, single-family home—thanks to savings from their net-lower mortgage payments—or renovate to incorporate the rental unit into the main house, which could be as simple as ripping out the kitchen and reconfiguring some of the space.

But it's important not to be too optimistic about the rent or the costs. You may not be able to get the rent you'd hoped for, and there may be months when the home sits vacant while you make upgrades and advertise for new tenants. Rather than figure on $1,000 a month forever, Michael Licamele, editor of MortgageAlmanac.com, advises that you budget at least one month of vacancy per year in good rental markets, and two to three months a year in softer markets. So in a good market a $1,000-a-month rental would generate an average $917 per month. He also recommends setting aside a small portion of each month's rental income for repairs.

You'll have to claim the rent as income, but you can deduct rental-related expenses, and your residence is excluded from stiffer capital gains taxes if you sell. You'll need an accountant to help sort it all out, and you should make sure the real estate agent is experienced in buying and selling multi-family homes.

Great Advice

Making Your House a Home— Not as Seen on TV

Now that you've got your house, how do you make it your castle? For the wealthy, the answer may be to hire a decorator and start signing the checks. Decorating a luxury home can run into the tens—or hundreds—of thousands of dollars. But most people aren't splurging on pricey rugs and gold-tinged wall hangings. Instead, having just put a chunk of savings into their biggest investment, typical buyers take things slowly, filling some rooms with new furniture and curtains and making do with what they have for others.

Before you get started, there are websites to help you design—even if you don't have an eye for what works. Consider YoungHouseLove.com's Mood Boards. You can browse through hundreds of designs, by color or by room, for all the rooms in your house. All the featured items are linked to sites where you can purchase them. Go to rd.com/home/decorating/diy-home-design-made-easy/.

Assessing the possibilities of what you've already got is key to a rich-looking home on a dime. "An old milk can could be transformed into a lamp, the base for a small table, an umbrella stand, or a planter. Be creative as you see each object's potential," according to Reader's Digest's *Penny Pincher's Almanac.*

Don't worry if you don't have loads of furniture. In decorating, less is often more, anyway. If you're using vibrant color on the walls and have an attractive rug picking up some of that color, you'll need only a few pieces of simple furniture, enlivened with a throw or some pillows, for a charming room. Bulky furniture can become obstacles for traffic flow through a room; it can create a cluttered feeling really fast; and it can detract from your one or two really good pieces.

Being smart about spending to decorate your home doesn't mean never splurging. Savvy homeowners can find ways to look like they live rich without spending a lot.

13 Ways to Get Designer Looks Without Paying a Fortune

1. Get thee to HomeGoods, Marshalls, or Ross. Lusting after that expensive lamp or elegant vase that you saw in the luxurious living room of the local Junior League? Dare you to pick it up next time. You're likely to find a partially peeled-off label from Marshalls or HomeGoods on the bottom. Designers say that while some rich clients insist on only pricey high-end items, many simply set a budget, says Amy McNenney, an interior designer who lives in the suburbs of New York City. Designers and decorators are more likely to put the bulk of it toward big items and find nice-looking replicas or less-pricey accent pieces at the same discount stores we all know and love. The result: a vase that looks like it costs $500 really costs just $50.

2. Find the clearance or outlet center of your favorite name-brand shops. Saks, Nordstrom, and Bloomingdale's all have outlet centers attached to their furniture or home stores. And many local furniture stores have a clearance room or floor. Shop them often. Most of the time, the products are first-rate—tags will indicate if they have flaws or are being sold as-is with some sort of defect—but may be overruns, floor samples, or returns. Often, you'll find the same exact rug, couch or dining room set in the clearance or outlet center as in the full-price side of the store—only for 25 to 60 percent less.

3. Shop showrooms for wallpaper and fabric. Fabric mills always have discontinued fabrics and wallpaper, often at 40 percent or more off wholesale. Call the corporate offices and ask if their showroom sales are open to the public. (Just make sure there's enough material in stock for your project.) Rug department stores mark up rugs 500 to 600 percent, so stick with wholesalers. Ask for references, a money-back guarantee, and free shipping.

4. Browse mid-level antique and thrift shops. One thing about decorating: People change their minds. And then they decide to sell a perfectly lovely buffet and hutch or rich leather couch online or via vintage shops or garage sales. Sometimes they just donate to thrift stores. McNenney says she's had some fabulous finds, including a Paul McCobb vintage dresser, which could sell for $600 to $1,000 at an antique store, for $60. She's

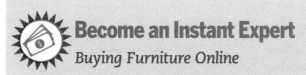

Become an Instant Expert
Buying Furniture Online

Before you purchase furniture online, keep in mind these 6 essential tips from *Reader's Digest*.

1. Ask for a swatch of fabric. See if it looks like it does in the picture. Do you like the feel? Does it seem durable?

2. Ask for a sample of the finish. Is it real wood? Is the color correct? Is it shiny or matte?

3. Does it look better online? If possible, visit a store that sells the pieces you're interested in so you can sit on and feel the furniture before you buy.

4. Check out assembly requirements. How long will it take to put together? If you need to hire someone to do it for you, figure out how much that will cost.

5. Ask about return policies. Do you have to pay for shipping? Furniture weighs a lot and will be expensive to return.

6. Check out the site you are shopping on with the Better Business Bureau. Read reviews to make sure it is a reputable site, especially if it's not a known name.

also purchased pricey vintage lamps for $30. And her favorite: a vintage love seat in crushed red velvet for $129. Once cleaned and the foam cushion replaced—for a few hundred dollars—she says it could have easily sold for up to $1,000 in a trendier vintage store. Be sure to give everything a good cleaning—especially furniture. She recommends keeping everything in a garage or outdoor space until you can clean or refinish it.

5. Go online. Craigslist and sites like it can be a treasure trove for buyers, too—with everything from Swedish couches to high-end bedroom sets for sale on any given day. Areas where there's a high tenant turnover—near colleges or apartment buildings—can be great places to find furniture, décor, and small appliances, says Freshome.com. And sites like stacksandstacks.com, Overstock.com, and others often sell quality wood furniture, wool rugs, and leather goods for 30 percent off or more. Be sure to read the reviews carefully to get a sense of quality, the merchant's responsiveness, and true-to-color issues.

6. Plan each room and buy high and low. McNenney recommends setting a budget for a room and sticking to it by going high and low: Buy several high-end pieces, and then accent everything else cheaply. "I believe in buying really solid upholstered pieces and tables, your base pieces, and then getting good deals on rugs and accents," says the interior designer. But that doesn't mean you should skip the thrift store. McNenney says the frame and woodwork on older pieces is often much better quality than newer items. "You may not save after refinishing the piece, but it's better quality," says McNenney. On the low end, she recommends buying lamps, sconces, wall hangings, and other accents at thrift and vintage stores or antique stores that are connected to church or hospital groups. For unique "low" finds, she suggests eBay or Etsy.

7. Display your photos creatively, with clips and magnets attached to metal bars. It's as easy as mounting two metal bars (about $8 each) on a wall or a door—or anywhere you have space—so you can display photos, postcards, or doodles. The best part is that the magnetic clips let you move the images around whenever you want. You could also opt for floating shelves—a set of three can cost less than $30 at a discount store—and choose slightly fancier picture frames purchased at a discounter like Marshalls or HomeGoods to give a room that splurged-on look for a cut-rate price.

8. Get creative with wall art. How about a wall hanging that catches the eye for $4.95? Frame gift wrapping from a store like Papyrus to create wall art. This stationery store—and others like it—create exquisite prints that are a welcome departure from the usual kitschy gift wraps. Choose one focal print, or mix and match a series of small prints, to liven up your bedroom walls. A frame from a discounter could leave your total for a new masterpiece in your living room at under $25.

9. Put a discount under your feet. Bring some Eastern flair to any room by visiting your favorite local carpet or rug store and asking about remnants to create area rugs. In many cases, other buyers change their minds about a pricey purchase, or a store—or customer—buys more rug than they need. What's leftover? A remnant piece that may be a size that's outside the norm or an irregular cut. Some rug stores will cut and bind remnants for free, and you'll pay up to 74 percent less than if you custom-ordered a rug. Other options: Pakobel Rugs eBay store. You'll find antique handmade rugs (Persian, Kashmiri, and more) at bargain prices. It's even possible to score a gorgeous rug for $40.

10. Kitchen facelifts for less. Don't like the color of your cabinets? You can reface your cabinets—and even if you have this done professionally, you will pay much less than it would cost to have new cabinets installed. You can save even more by doing the refacing yourself. This usually involves gluing new veneer over the old finish on all the vertical surfaces. You can get the veneer and instructions at home centers. You can also get new cabinet doors and drawer fronts to replace your old ones, refinishing the cabinet frame before installing the new doors and drawer fronts. A less-intensive option: Take off all the cabinet doors and drawers and paint a brand-new look. You can also buy new knobs, handles, and drawer pulls, which can give a kitchen a different look. Many can be found at local hardware stores, and more interesting options are often a staple of vintage and antique stores.

11. Focus on fixtures. A complete bathroom renovation is pricey, but simply switching out your old fixtures— faucets, showerhead, and knobs—is an easy and relatively inexpensive way to upgrade. Bonus: New showerheads can be more efficient, so you'll save on your water bill, too.

12. Learn to do it yourself. A great way to save money on a designer look is to learn to do many of the installations yourself. There are a number of books you can borrow or buy to learn techniques, but sometimes a class can make what you want to do really clear. Check with your local home center for classes (free or for the cost of materials) in laying tile, painting techniques, and more. You can check with a university nearby to see what extension classes it offers, or if you learn well from the web, there are videos out there for just about any how-to project.

13. Get an expert plan. If you can't afford a landscaper to plan and plant your dream garden, hire someone to do a landscape design and then install it yourself in stages. You'll avoid potentially costly mistakes, like putting the forsythia bushes in the wrong place and having to move or, worse, replace them later. Such plans can cost as little as $100 in many areas.

13 Things Rich People Won't Tell You about Their Home

1. Most of it is off-limits. Many of the super-wealthy have huge homes with specific rooms dedicated to entertaining. The rest of the house is off-limits, says Ryan Serhant, a real estate broker and star of *Million Dollar Listing New York* on Bravo television. Your home might not have a ballroom, but you can save yourself stress by having your own off-limits areas when entertaining. Bonus: You can shove the "I don't know what to do with this stuff" pile in one of those rooms and shut the door.

2. They don't get emotionally attached. Serhant says the most interesting contrast between the super-rich and the other homebuyers is what he calls "walk-away power." If the price goes above their predetermined limit, "even if they feel it is the most perfect home in the world, they simply walk away," Serhant says. The power to walk away without losing anything is the strongest negotiating position—one that any buyer should keep in mind. And even when the wealthy walk away from a home they love, they don't look back. "They realize the value of their money and view property more as an investment than as a place to feel warm and cozy," says Serhant.

3. They get mortgages even when they could pay cash. Remember those perks that banks give the wealthy? Among them are very flexible home loans at interest rates even better than the lows the rest of us have seen in recent years, because the rich are the least risky borrowers. "It might make more sense to keep the cash in other investments," says Serhant. While everyday millionaires may still derive a lot of their money from their work, Serhant says the super-rich keep a good portion of their money in hedge funds because of potentially outsized returns that can hit 10 percent or more. So even if a mortgage rate is 2 percent, a wealthy buyer is still making quite a bit more by keeping that money where it is instead of cashing out funds to pay for a house.

4. They don't spend enough time thinking about the neighbors. Those noisy or messy neighbors—be it loud parties, exotic pets that howl at all hours, one project car after another in the driveway, or low-brow landscaping—the quality of the neighbors affects a home's value and your enjoyment of your home, explains Madison Hildebrand, a Malibu, California, real estate agent and a star of Bravo's *Million Dollar Listing Los Angeles* show. Hildebrand himself says that his next-door neighbor has parrots that shriek loudly as early as 5:00 A.M. Annoying for the average homeowner. But, he says, rich buyers often regret not paying more attention to their neighbors. Of course, neighborly regret isn't limited to the rich, so spend some time observing the neighbor's yard and habits before you buy. Stop by on a weekend, after work, and in the morning to get a sense of life on either side—and behind—the house you want.

5. They want a bigger, better, newer one than the Joneses. Yes, the Joneses have their own set of mega-Joneses they feel compelled to keep up with, explains Serhant. "Everything's relative," he says. "Does anyone really need 18 bedrooms and 25 bathrooms over 20,000 square feet on 5 acres? The answer speaks for itself." It's easy to get caught up in the don't-have thinking at any price point, whether it's 18 bedrooms or 5 instead of the 3 you really need. But the rich, well, they're already loaded up with a lot of extra zeros in their bank accounts. On your way to the club, remind yourself of your own needs—not your neighbor's.

6. They sweat the small stuff. The rich address repairs immediately and aggressively, says Serhant, because they view their home as an investment. Like any investment, it's critical to ensure that the fundamentals are—and remain—solid. "You won't find a piece of wallpaper curling, even in the bathroom," quips Hildebrand. Consider your own home-buying expeditions. The value of a home immediately drops in the eyes of any buyer when simple repairs and maintenance are undone. The next natural question: If the stuff I can see isn't taken care of, what about the stuff I can't see? Make sure you have a repair fund. Maintain the value of your biggest investment and use it on the little things before they become big things.

7. They rarely have buyer's remorse. Serhant says that wealthier clients tend to be very analytical with their money and how they spend it. It's how they've amassed their fortune, Serhant says, and it's how they manage their money when buying a home—or anything else.

8. They get greedy. The wealthiest of buyers didn't get that way by paying full price. And they buy homes no differently, often driving a hard bargain on prices. "They'll try to get a bigger discount [than the average homebuyer]," shares Hildebrand. Rich buyers often insist on certain features—saunas, home gyms, and more—that they barely utilize once they've moved in.

9. Rich people are smarter about their privacy than you are. "When they make their initial offer, they will include a confidentiality agreement," explains Hildebrand. "That prevents the agent and the people involved in the transaction sharing information about the deal." You can ask for the same when you make an initial offer on a property. Why bother? It not only protects your personal information but protects your initial offer from being exploited by other buyers, says Hildebrand, who could swoop in and outbid you or, worse, drive up the price.

10. They sometimes pay seller's closing costs. While many wealthy buyers will take a mortgage to preserve their investment income, sometimes they'll cover the seller's closing costs by paying the seller's real estate agent's commission. That reduces the home's price and can save a significant amount in real estate taxes. If you can afford it and it makes sense to you, there's no reason not to do the same. "You're saving yourself the money," adds Hildebrand.

11. They don't consider the cost of their McMansion's upkeep. A big home on an expansive piece of property requires a lot of maintenance. And for the wealthy, that often means having a number of people at their home practically every day. The gardener, the cook, the housekeeper, the security, the dog walker, the assistant . . . all that personnel really adds up. It is important to consider the amount of upkeep a home will involve. A large lawn needs to be mowed. A 15-foot-ceilinged great room is beautiful but can raise your utility bills by 15 percent, say experts. Consider these expenses—and whether you can, say, mow the lawn yourself or absorb the higher electric bill—when considering a home.

12. It's what's on the outside that counts. It's not just the interior decorating that matters. Especially after the recession, "I've seen people take a Tuscan home and transform it into a modern home," says Hildebrand. "They've done exterior and interior complete remodels." Some spend millions on the renovations, but that's still less than they'd pay in taxes and other expenses to buy a new home to their style liking. But there's an upside to doing even modest exterior renovations. Adding simple (even do-it-yourself) stonework along an entry pathway, upgrading steps and handrails, updating worn siding, and improving landscaping can add tremendous curb appeal when you're selling a house—plus, it's a prettier scene to come home to.

13. They still shop at Target. Okay, some do. Hildebrand says that some clients love to shop at Target, Macy's, and other mid-level or discount stores. "Not everybody was born rich, and some people grew up going to those types of places and they still love to get a good deal," he explains. The rich didn't get that way by spending $50 on an item they could get for $25 at a discount store. But, says Hildebrand, when it comes to things their guests will see or use (like bedsheets, guest bath towels) they're likely to pick up higher-end items from pricier stores.

Great Advice

6 Things New Homeowners Wish They'd Known before Buying

You've just been handed the keys to your new-to-you home, and the movers are on their way. It's the first joy of home ownership: making the new place your own. And then the little bits of reality set in and you wonder—much like the early days of parenthood—*why didn't anyone ever tell me about this part?* That's especially true, since these I-never-knewisms usually involve money. So to spare you the reality check, here are a few things that new homeowners wish they'd known.

1. Budget for at least $2,000 per year in expenses. That includes $50 to $100 a month for routine maintenance. Inevitably, a repair that looked like it could wait a few years will need to be fixed right away—and it probably won't be cheap. Something as simple as a new water heater could cost upward of $1,000; a busted plumbing pipe could be a cheap fix or cost hundreds of dollars to repair. Keep a separate home-maintenance fund for these things that pop up and need to be taken care of right away. And expect to shell out up to $100, and perhaps more in pricier locales, for the little things, like replacing a mailbox post that's suddenly looking a little rotted, replacing cracked patio pavers, or treating for pests or weeds.

2. The sidewalk is probably your responsibility. If you are used to living in a big city or have been a longtime renter, don't be surprised when you have to shovel your own snow. What's more, many towns require homeowners to maintain the sidewalks and will issue tickets—with strict deadlines before fines increase—if they deem your sidewalk in need of repair. It may be as simple as filling in cracks or involve replacing each sidewalk panel to the tune of several hundred dollars per. Homeowners in an association may not have as much responsibility for the sidewalk out front, but check policies before you buy.

3. Yes, your fees are going up. We need new sidewalks and better landscaping at the clubhouse. Living in a gated community or within the rules of a homeowners association has upsides like better-maintained streets, a community pool, and clubhouse and security. But, in addition to annual HOA fees, you could find yourself paying an extra assessment for big repairs or upgrades that you don't have much say about. Ask about the history of assessments, how they're doled out to homeowners, and who, exactly, decides what needs to be done.

4. The sellers patched and sealed and painted, but not to your liking. Repairs or upgrades could just be on the surface to get the home looking good to secure a quick sale. You may find that holes in a wall weren't patched properly or that the porch railings were given a fresh coat of paint but not the weather-resistant, outdoor kind. Anticipate the need to upgrade or "fix" small things around the house to correct the corrections. A few weekend hours will usually do the trick, and a good home inspector will find anything that's truly problematic (in other words, costly to fix).

5. Maintaining a lawn and landscape is harder—and pricier—than you think. That's especially true if you make a mistake—like, say, under- or overwatering your lawn. One inch of water once a week is ideal, maybe once every five days in extreme heat, depending on your soil. Infrequent, soaking watering encourages roots to grow deeper. And it doesn't stop with the grass. Plants need to be pruned and mulch—which can cost $4 to $10 a bag— spread. New bulbs and flowers can add up fast. Shop big-box home-improvement stores like Home Depot or Lowes to find bargains that can be mixed in with more expensive landscape purchases. Experts say you should expect to pay $20 to $40 per square foot for landscape design and basic landscaping, half that if you do most of it yourself.

6. Your property taxes will only go up. Even if the value of your home goes down year after year, it's a safe bet that your property taxes will go up nonetheless. If values go down, so do town coffers—so the tax increases will just be higher to make up for it. School-related property taxes are a full 60 percent of most homeowners' tax bills, and you'll likely get a chance to vote on any increases. But remember, good schools contribute to home values, so many school budget increases pass muster with voters. Expect your property taxes to rise, on average, by a few percent per year—more in pricier locales.

Who Knew?
Worth-It Renovations

. . . .

Realtor to the rich Serhant says wealthy homeowners tend to spend quite a bit on renovations and customizations. "To them it's more about making the home their own than the investment they make on renovations," he says. That means they're not thinking foremost about a return on the money they put into a home, partly because they bought shrewdly to start.

But for most homeowners who would eventually like to sell their homes, adding value while personalizing a home requires a mix of dreaming and common sense—lest you end up with a big-ticket renovation with little or no return down the road.

How to know? Here are the projected returns on investment (ROI) for some popular renovations, according to *Remodeling* magazine's 2013 "Cost vs. Value" report. The value of various improvements depends on where you live—basements add more return on investment in some parts of the country, while attic bedrooms offer more in others—as well as the value of homes in the region and how much buyers in an area look for certain features (what they are willing to fork over extra money for).

Expanding Living Space with a Basement or Attic Renovation

Turning an attic into a bedroom or remodeling a basement into a living space have higher-than-average returns. You'll likely recoup 72.9 percent of an attic conversion's cost and 70.3 percent on a basement renovation when you sell. In Washington, D.C., that attic bedroom has a massive ROI of nearly 92 percent, and the ROI is 83.3 percent for the basement remodel. But in Cincinnati your ROI sinks to just 62.7 percent on the attic and 55.3 percent for the basement project.

Remodeling magazine's report points out that these projects have higher average costs—$47,919 for the attic and $61,303 for the basement—but "are still the least expensive way for homeowners to add living space."

If Only We Had Another Bathroom . . .

A mid-range bathroom addition costs $37,500, on average. But the return on investment averages only 54.8 percent, so you will want to carefully consider how badly you want and need the extra room. The payoff depends partly on how many bathrooms you already have: going from one to two bathrooms in a 3-bedroom house will return more than going from three to four bathrooms. And location counts—in the Midwest, ROI slips to just over 43 percent.

But remodeling an existing bathroom costs less and pays more. On average, a basic job costs just $15,780 and returns 65 percent—more if you're going from, say, one and a half bathrooms to two full baths in that

3-bedroom home. But a bathroom remodel in New Haven, Connecticut, will have a lower ROI, of just 51.4 percent.

Overhauling Your Kitchen

A minor kitchen remodel, such as replacing cabinet fronts, countertops, hardware, and appliances without making any major structural changes, nets one of the highest returns on investment, about 75.4 percent. That's a great deal, considering the relatively low cost: an average $18,527 nationally, according to the report. ROI shoots up to over 99 percent in San Diego, California, but is far lower—66.1 percent—in Indianapolis, Ind.

The average price tag of a mid-range full kitchen renovation for 2013—gutting the interior and upgrading everything—was nearly $54,000 nationally, but your ROI is closer to 69 percent, depending on where you live. In Des Moines, Iowa, and Tampa, Florida, your costs would be a few thousand dollars less, but you'll recoup vastly different amounts—a meager 57 percent in Des Moines vs. 74 percent of your costs in Tampa. In certain neighborhoods a dated kitchen can kill your home's chances for a quick sale. Indeed, in cases where upgraded kitchens are considered standard by homebuyers, a kitchen renovation could return more than 100 percent, according to the National Association of Realtors.

A New Family Room off the Back

Be prepared to pay $79,000, on average nationally, to add more space for the family. And unless your house lacks space to begin with, you likely won't get more than a 63 percent return on your investment. You'll see an even lower ROI in Worcester, Massachusetts—just 58.6 percent—and a higher one in a city like Tampa or San Diego—67.4 percent and 79.8 percent, respectively—where spacious homes are in demand.

Of course, if your goal is to have somewhere to watch television and a playroom for the kids, the ROI on the extra space might not matter so much. And if extra space is a must-have in your town, your returns could be higher.

SOURCE: HSH.com.

Big Tip!
A Home Remodeling Checklist from *Reader's Digest*

· ·

There is no doubt about it: Just planning a renovation can be time-consuming and stressful—hunting down a contractor, pursuing construction permits, securing the financing. Here are some remodeling prep tips from home-repair expert Mike Holmes, star of HGTV's *Holmes on Homes,* to help you get started.

PLAN: KNOW YOUR NEEDS

Do your homework. Start with a list of preferences for such items as lighting, flooring, and appliances—and include brand names. This will keep you and your general contractor on the same page about the costs and quality of the work. The more details you can provide, the better.

Put your ideas on paper. Make sketches and draw up floor plans to discuss with your contractor. It's best to have an idea for him to work with rather than start with a blank slate.

BUDGET: CONTROL SPENDING

Don't just decide on which products you want your contractor to use. Call around for estimates for how much they cost to install. Factor these in, along with miscellaneous expenses such as dining out or booking a hotel room when and if construction makes the space temporarily unlivable. This leads to a realistic budget.

Plan to spend more than you think. A good rule of thumb is to set aside 10 to 15 percent more than you figure your renovation will cost.

HIRE: ASK THE RIGHT QUESTIONS
Important questions to ask the contractor include:

* What warranty do you offer, and what does it cover?

* May I see a copy of your business license?

* Are you going to acquire the correct permits for the job or should I?

4

The Financial Road to Higher Education

Think your kid should help pay for college? You're thinking like a rich person: A whopping 72 percent of wealthy families—those with more than $250,000 to invest—think their child should pay at least part of the bill, and nearly a third think the prospective student should contribute at least half, according to a 2012 survey of 1,000 affluent families by asset manager Legg Mason. That's hardly small change: the average annual cost of a four-year private college is $38,600 for tuition, fees, and room and board; in-state costs for a public school averages $17,130 per year, according to the College Board.

Sixty percent of students take out loans to help pay for college, says the Associated Press—which isn't necessarily a bad thing. Students who pay for part of their education and have some "skin in the game" may work harder in college, according to a study in the American Sociological Review. The study also found that students with access to lots of mom-and-dad money tend to socialize more and have lower grades.

While the wealthy can often afford to foot most of the bill, the rest of us—and our kids—can't write out a $30,000 check. While college debt is nearly impossible to avoid, a bit of smart planning and rich-guy thinking can keep the burden manageable.

13 Things Rich People Won't Tell You about College Planning and Saving

1. I push my kids to the schools that really want them. Some elite private universities and Ivy League schools really, really want not-so-rich kids and will help make paying for a pricey education easier. "More and more top schools are recognizing that their lack of income diversity is a serious problem," writes independent college counselor David Montesano in a blog post for thecollegesolution.com. Ivy League schools and other pricey, private universities, like Amherst College, are offering grants instead of loans in their financial-aid packages to attract talented students who might be turned off by their sticker price. Other schools use a sliding scale that substantially limits borrowing and replaces it with grants, even for families with incomes just over $100,000. And some require no contribution from families earning under $50,000 or $60,000 per year.

$ TOP SECRET! Look at what aid is available at your child's target colleges—particularly if they're pricey private schools; you might be surprised that because your income is, say, $75,000 per year, you will only be asked to contribute 10 percent of whatever the federal formula suggests you should. "No matter how much you save, you have to look at what resources the colleges and universities have," says John Myers, Delaware high school guidance counselor and father of four. "A school with a good endowment will give you more money, both school- and need-based." That means a more expensive school might actually leave you with less to pay out of pocket simply because it has more to give in the first place.

2. I have a plan. More than half of families earning $100,000 a year or more had a college savings plan in place before their child entered college, compared with only 37 percent of families earning $35,000 to $100,000 a year, according to a 2012 study by Sallie Mae, which annually measures how American families pay for college. Planning ahead isn't just smart budgeting; it's the kind of rich-guy vision that sets expectations, forces you to think about how to pay before you have to, and creates a cash reserve to pay the bill.

3. Junior's room and board is on my Amex. Wealthier families are twice as likely to pay for college costs with credit cards and to take bigger private student loans, Sallie Mae found. But if you're not among the wealthy, you can do what most of your richer counterparts don't: Use a home-equity loan or line of credit to pay for college. For families with significant equity in their homes—and you will be one if you applied that rich-guy vision to your home buying—ultra-low rates can provide a source of low-interest cash to round out paying the bill. A home-equity loan can be had at low interest rates these days, compared to double-digit rates for credit cards and high single-digit rates for private loans. Just be sure not to borrow more than your budget allows or cut into retirement savings to make the payments.

4. I recruit a LOT of my young employees from public universities, not pricier private schools. Students should consider applying to the 20 percent of top public colleges, says Montesano, which can be 50 percent cheaper than private colleges. Want your kid to get hired right out of college? Many companies believe the quality and potential of public school graduates outpaces that of, say, Ivy League schools, a 2010 *Wall Street Journal* survey found. Sitting at the top of the list: Pennsylvania State University, University of Wisconsin-Madison, Ohio State University, University of Florida, and two University of California schools, among others.

5. Merit scholarships don't care about how much money you make—and we apply for as many as we can. Wealthier families get about the same share of scholarships and grants that middle-income families do, Sallie Mae found, but families earning more than $100,000 a year got bigger grants: an average $8,700 in 2012, vs. $7,046 for middle-income families. Most aren't based on need; the broad pot of merit scholarships is available to everyone. You can take advantage of them, too, by searching sites like CollegeBoard.com and FastWeb.com.

6. Smart savings can cover a lot of the costs. About 26 percent of college costs are paid out of parents' savings and income—for wealthier families it jumps to 42 percent. So with your rich-guy vision you can benefit from saving more sooner to make the tuition burden a little lighter later. Start your 529 plan as soon as your child is born or as soon as you can afterward, recommends Mark Kantrowitz, publisher of FinAid.org and FastWeb.com, two leading resources on college aid, savings, and scholarships. Withdrawals from these state-sponsored plans to pay for education are tax-free, and there are often state tax deductions that can be useful as a child nears college age. You can also now pay for your child's college computer and other technology-related expenses via 529 funds.

7. It pays to have help to find scholarships and get admitted. For the wealthiest of families, it's worth a few thousand dollars to hire a service to find obscure scholarships, or up to $40,000 for an elite college admissions counselor. But there are plenty of free resources to find grants and scholarships. FinAid.org is one of the most comprehensive. Sure, it may take a few hours to search the databases and up to five hours to fill out each application, but just think: For 20 hours spent over a few weeks, your child could score a few thousand dollars to offset the cost of tuition. As for admissions counselors, you don't always have to be left out in the cold—although it still won't be cheap.

Become an Instant Expert
Become a Scholarship Queen (or King)

Finding scholarships is a little bit art, a little bit science, and lot of digging and personal effort. Don't be dismayed. It's worth the effort, say guidance counselors and parents. The reason: Many, many people who would qualify for scholarships simply never apply. That leaves the field wide open for everyone else—namely, those who will take the time to apply even for the $250 and $500 scholarships.

Think it's not worth it to spend an hour or two applying for a few hundred dollars of scholarship money? Think again. "If you do not apply for a scholarship, you do not get the scholarship," says Delaware high school gidance couselor John Myers. He and Louis Barajas, a financial adviser from Irvine, California, say you'd be surprised at how few people actually apply for scholarships. So even if you are sure that Jane Valedictorian applied for the local Rotary Cub scholarship and she's sure to win it, she may not have. But you very well could if you apply.

Sometimes it can make all the difference. Myers tells the story of Tori, a student who graduated about five years ago. "We called her the scholarship queen," Myers said. And it's no wonder. Her mother, Cindy, says she went to the guidance office every chance she got to dig for scholarships that might not have been on databases.

"She applied for every scholarship she could, even if they were just for $250," Cindy said. "When she graduated, at the awards ceremony she had the most scholarships of anyone. It was nowhere near where some kids were moneywise, but the $250 here and $1,000 there really added up."

Tori graduated from Virginia Tech. "She would not have been able to go to school if she didn't get the scholarships," says Myers. Tori began digging through scholarship books again in 2013, Cindy said, to help fund a graduate degree after she was accepted into University of North Carolina's speech pathology program.

Many elite consultants—those with 90 percent or better admissions rates—have junior employees for half the price, and admissions consultants whose names aren't bandied about by the country-club set often charge even less. Ask for recommendations from friends or guidance counselors at your child's high school.

8. Know your tax loopholes, err, advantages. The wealthy have many ways to leverage tax reductions to offset college costs but often earn too much to qualify for education-related tax credits and deductions that most middle-class taxpayers can take advantage of. The American Opportunity tax credit can reduce your federal tax bill by $2,500 for each qualifying student— or $200-plus more in your paycheck to help fund school each month. The Lifetime Learning Credit can add back up to $2,000 per year. And for those who don't qualify for these credits, the IRS allows deductions that can total up to $4,000 for tuition and other expenses. And, of course, there are often tax advantages to saving in a 529 plan in your state.

9. Boot camp—it's for college prep, too. Vermont college admissions consultant Michele Hernandez charges families upward of $42,000 to coach their children through high school and the college admissions process, with acceptance rates at choice schools of 90 to 95 percent. A tad out of your price range? Hernandez and consultants across the country also offer summer boot camps that teach kids how to best highlight themselves in their college applications.

The most prestigious can run between $8,000 and $15,000 per person and are typically a week long. And some local guidance organizations and a number of less-costly admissions consulting groups offer lower-cost summer programs and on-demand online boot camps for under $1,000.

10. Work isn't a dirty word—so we do more of it. A full 20 percent of high-income families—and about the same number of middle-income earners—work more to help pay for their child's education, Sallie Mae found. In some cases a spouse who worked part-time bumped up to full-time, or a stay-at-home parent got part-time work. It's not exactly an easy equation if you already work a full-time job. But consider your skill set and whether or not you can squeeze in side projects here and there or log a bit more overtime to, say, help cover the costs of books or a meal plan for the school year. Freelance job-connection websites like Odesk.com and Guru.com can connect you with short-duration or short-hours projects that can often be done in non-work hours. Oh, and 42 percent of wealthier families said that their child worked more to offset college costs—not too far behind the 51 percent of middle-income families that said the same.

11. I might not get it, but I always apply for financial aid. Consider this: 72 percent of high-income families apply for financial aid, according to the Sallie Mae study, even though they don't always get much, if any. If a second child starts college while a first is still studying, that no-aid letter could turn into an award, albeit small. The lesson: It can't hurt to try.

12. When I don't qualify for school-based financial aid, there's more for you, especially at colleges with a lot of rich kids. Nearly half of upper- and middle-class families receive college grants—up from just 30 percent a decade ago. Most wealthy families won't qualify for the sort of need-based aid that individual universities hand out to round out federal aid or replace loans (those are given to families earning under a certain amount—sometimes as high as $100,000 per year but usually for those earning under $65,000 per year). So colleges are giving out more aid from their own coffers to middle-class families—including loan-replacement grants targeted at needier families.

13. Faster and nearby is just fine—and maybe cheaper. A full 24 percent of high-income earners save on college costs by having their child finish college faster. Students who double up on courses for a year or study part-time during the summer—often at lower-cost institutions with transferrable credits—can graduate a semester or even a year early, saving tens of thousands of dollars. The College Board recently noted that more college applicants—and colleges—expressed interest in three-year degrees. Nearly half of higher-income families said their child lived at home for at least some of their college years—another big savings at a time when room and board at a state school averages over $9,000 per year and more at private universities.

Great Advice
Savings Isn't Enough

John Myers has helped thousands of high schoolers maneuver their way through college applications over his 36 years as a guidance counselor at a Delaware high school.

When it came to saving for college for his four children, he and his wife—a teacher—opened 529 plans and set aside savings bonds from relatives; a life insurance policy from Myers's mother provided a $90,000 windfall. The Myerses received it when their oldest child was still preschool-age, and they planned to let that money grow to help pay for each child's first two years of college.

When their oldest, Chris, graduated in 1999, the plan looked to be working. "The first and second year we were able to write a check," said Myers. "But then the stock market crashed." Suddenly the account's value fell to $60,000, and there wasn't much time before the next child, Brian, was off to college. "Close to $40,000 we had counted on was gone, and it was going to take a long time to build that back up," he says. Chris took out federal loans.

Brian decided to go to school in-state, a virtually free option, giving the Myerses time to recover. It also gave them time to have conversations with their children about the sacrifices they would have to make—taking loans, digging for and applying for scholarships, and working part-time.

"When the third was ready for college, we had built back some of that money," Myers says. Third child Scott also received some scholarships and financial aid, and the Myerses were able to write a check to cover the difference for freshman and sophomore years. But by junior year the well had run dry and Scott had to take federal loans.

For their youngest child, Daniel, who'll graduate from high school in spring 2014, the Myerses won't have any money left. They refinanced their mortgage to pay off private loans they'd taken for the other children, as well as a small portion of the private loans that two of their children took during college—and say they'll do the same for Daniel if they can. They've told Daniel that he'll have to take on a bigger portion of loans to pay for school. "In the long run, you do get your bang for your buck and the loans are worth it, but initially it's really scary," he says.

Even if you save smart and have some money in the bank to help pay for college, you should expect to take out some sort of private loans and anticipate that your child will take out loans.

"If you think your child might go to a four-year university, you have to find a way to start saving the day they are born. But from a reality standpoint, that may not even make a big enough difference, because a top-level liberal arts school is going to cost $50,000 easy," says Myers.

13 Tricks of the
Financial Aid Trade

1. Apply for every scholarship you qualify for. It doesn't matter if it's for $500 and the essay will take you an hour to write. If you win, you just got $500 for an hour of work. "The people you hear about who win gazillions in scholarship all have one thing in common," says Mark Kantrowitz, the publisher of FinAid.org and FastWeb.com and a leading authority on saving for and paying for college. "They applied for every scholarship for which they were eligible."

2. Look offline. Local or smaller scholarships may not be in a database. Look for them in your guidance counselor's office or at the financial aid office of a local college. Some of the awards may be smaller, but there will be fewer people applying, since the criteria will be narrow. Small, local awards like a PTA scholarship don't want to be listed in a database, because they want to limit the number of applicants.

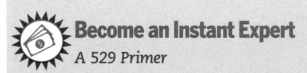

Become an Instant Expert
A 529 Primer

Simply put, 529s are state-sponsored, tax-advantaged savings plans for future college costs. The most available and popular are college savings plans.

A parent, grandparent, relative, or friend sets up the account to pay the prospective student's future tuition and selects how the plan should invest the money—mutual or moneymaker funds, etc. The money your investments earn are free from federal and often state taxes, so long as you use withdrawals for eligible college expenses, such as tuition and room and board. Many states offer tax or other benefits to residents, such as matching grants, for investing in a 529 plan while you are still investing the money—you know, when Junior is 10 years old and still eight years away from attending college.

You can open a 529 plan through an adviser, but often at a high fee, which can eat into your returns. In many states, you can buy a no-fee plan directly from a plan sponsor or plan. The College Savings Plan, collegesavings.org, is a good starting point for these, and to compare plans, tax advantages, and performance of funds in different states. In some cases a plan in another state may have advantages—more investment options, lower fees, better long-term performance—that outweigh tax benefits offered by 529s in your home state. Mark Kantrowitz, of FinAid.org, recommends only direct-sold plans with fees below 1 percent. He says Fidelity, Vanguard, and TIAA-CREF have been in a bit of a price war, driving down fees to as low as half a percent. The less you pay in fees, the more of your returns go to tuition.

Certain she'll attend a private university? Look into private college 529 plans; privatecollege529.com lets you lock in today's tuition prices for up to 30 years by buying semester tuition certificates for participating schools—no matter how much tuition rises or what happens in the financial markets. Right now a semester tuition certificate costs about $10,000 and can be used at any of the 270 participating schools. The plan guarantees that the school will accept the lower payment down the road.

3. Behold the FAFSA. Fill it out fast, early, every year. The Free Application for Federal Student Aid is the key to federal, state, and, usually, college-given financial aid, since it determines the amount a family can reasonably be expected to contribute for college costs. Fill it out as close to January 1 as possible, using the prior year's last pay stub to estimate taxable income figures. You'll be asked to update it after you file your tax returns. Fill it out every year, even if you get no aid one year. "The formula is complicated and it changes, so it is hard to figure out if you qualify," Kantrowitz, says.

4. Consider your assets. Financial aid formulas look first to tap a child's savings account to help pay for college, so try to keep savings in a parental account. Aid formulas then move to 529 savings, which offset the amount of aid you qualify for—but that's still better than footing a bigger bill. If you have a credit card balance of a few thousand dollars and have the cash to pay it off, do it. You're saving 14 percent credit card interest, but better yet, you're reducing your "assets" by the same amount, which matters when it comes to your aid award calculation.

5. Go federal for loans first. Federal loans have fixed rates, while most private loans have variable rates, so they have nowhere to go but up. A few lenders offer fixed-rate, fixed-term loans, but they tend to come with slightly higher interest rates and are offered only to borrowers with the best credit scores. And some require repayment starting before graduation. "Most people are better off with federal education loans," says Kantrowitz. They are typically cheaper and have better repayment terms—including, in some cases, forgiveness in exchange for public service.

6. Brace yourself and your kid for more debt. Myers, the Delaware guidance counselor, says that even if you save smartly and put aside a windfall, you should anticipate taking out some loans and have a frank talk with your children about taking out their own loans. Most schools only let students take out about $20,000 in federal student loans over four years. "Consider that a new car costs $20,000 or $25,000 and it seems more manageable," he says. "And you have more time to pay off student loans than you do a car."

7. Your retirement funds are just for you. Resist the temptation to divert your retirement contributions to the college fund—and don't even think about raiding your 401(k) so your kid won't have to borrow as much. "There's no guarantee the children will help you down the road," notes Myers, echoing advice by many financial planners. "You have to secure your retirement even if it means your kids take more student loans."

8. Open that 529 on the way home from the hospital. When should you start saving, and how much should you save? As soon as a child is born, and as much as you can. Kantrowitz says it's smart to save $250 per child per month if you expect him to go to a state university in 17 years and $500 if you think a private school is in Junior's future. But you can start by saving even $25 a month and upping the contribution over time, meaning you'll have to borrow less later.

9. But before investing, do your homework. A 529 plan will generally cut down on the amount of financial aid available to a student, and the tax advantages and investment options vary. Even so, saving for years means you've got the money in hand and haven't missed it so much. If you don't have the savings, you'll be stuck with the bill all at once. What's more, 529 savings don't completely wipe out aid, since colleges consider the amount not just for use the first year.

10. Reserve that windfall. Each time you get a raise, a windfall, or an expense off your plate, increase what you save for college, Kantrowitz recommends. Baby finally out of diapers? Put that $50 a month toward the college savings plan. Done with day care? Put part of that money into the college savings plan.

11. Rack up rewards points. By signing up for set-and-forget rewards programs like Upromise and giving your credit and store reward card numbers, you add a little something to your college savings plan without much work—$100 to $150 a year. Friends, relatives, and godparents can all sign up, too, adding to the pot.

12. Is the army life for your kid? If you're interested in the military, consider ROTC scholarships, which can

Become an Instant Expert
Free Ways to Find Free Money

Scholarship America, a national organization that helps students get into and graduate from college, recommends these free sites for scholarship searches:

CollegeBoard.org: Its scholarship database contains more than 2,300 scholarship opportunities, totaling nearly $3 billion.

CollegeNet.com: A scholarship search engine and social network in which students create topics, participate in discussions, and vote on which participant is leading the most interesting conversation. By the end of the voting cycle every Wednesday, the student with the most votes wins $3,000 to $5,000 in scholarship money.

FastWeb.com: The first online scholarship matching service and free national scholarship matching service has helped 50 million students find money since its founding 15 years ago. It has 1.5 million scholarships worth $3.4 billion in its database. It also includes a comprehensive questionnaire to help match your specifics (born in that no-name town in the South? At least one-eighth French?) to available scholarships.

Scholarships.com: The site says it is the largest free and independent scholarship search and financial aid information resource, with more than 2.7 million scholarships worth a total of $19 billion in its database.

ScholarshipMonkey.com: The site has access to more than 1 million undergraduate, graduate, and professional scholarship awards worth in excess of $3 billion from greater than 4,000 sources.

cover a huge chunk of college costs in exchange for spending several years in the military after graduation.

13. Don't get overwhelmed. Financial aid and paying for college can seem like a foreign language and can be intimidating, but what you need to do is really not so intimidating, Kantrowitz says. "Families get worried not about what they know, but what they don't know. The key is to not panic, because the process is relatively simple to follow."

If you save $200 a month for 10 years at 6.8 percent return— about the average return— you'll have about $34,400 toward college, Kantrowitz notes. But if you borrow the same amount and pay it back over 10 years at 6.8 percent interest rate, it'll cost you $396 a month.

$ TOP SECRET! Start searching for scholarships before senior year of high school and answer all the optional questions on a scholarship-matching questionnaire; these dictate what awards you're shown. If you win a renewable scholarship, be sure to find out what you must do to renew it—missing a simple essay on what you did during the school year can jeopardize getting the award again. And any scholarship you have to pay to get is probably a scam.

Great Advice
Starting Smarter

The Sallie Mae study of how Americans pay for college revealed another trick many more families are using to use their college dollars more wisely: Some 29 percent said their child was enrolled at a community college, compared to 23 percent in 2010. But few of those kids will likely stay in community college to graduate. The most ambitious students know a good thing when they see it: Go for the cheaper tuition, get the basics out of the way, and transfer to the big-name university after a year or two. Since community college tuition is just a few thousand dollars per year, that can mean a huge savings.

"It doesn't matter where you start; it matters where you finish," explains Myers. "If the best place for you to start is at a branch campus [of a large university] or somewhere tuition-free or inexpensive like a community college and then transfer, you should do that."

Financial adviser Louis Barajas says that at the end of the day, parents want happy, healthy kids who will use that education to better their lives. "Part of education planning is opening a 529 to save, but part of it is saying 'I want what's best for you, my child,' and maybe what's best is a part-time job and a year or two at community college while he figures out what he wants and where to apply to school next," says Barajas.

Become an Instant Expert
Upromise, You Get Money for College

Want a little free money for college? Upromise, which launched in 2001, allows you to link credit and rewards cards to a Upromise account and earn 1 percent to 25 percent back on a wide range of qualified purchases.

Those earnings can be used toward college tuition and costs, says Upromise, as well as classes to make a career change or upgrade your skills, get a certification, learn a language, or go back to school.

The money is contributed by participating merchants, who sometimes offer bonus earnings during the year. What's in it for them? They hope that you'll become a loyal customer by earning a few dollars toward college costs.

Some families may only earn $100 per year, but others can make significantly more. For instance, get a Groupon deal via the Upromise link for $50 and earn 5 percent back—now times that by 10 per year and you've earned $25. Now add in gas, groceries, and dinners out and it's easy to see how the (free) college savings can add up.

There are some strings. For example, if you shop online, you have to click through to participating merchants from the Upromise website. If you eat at a participating restaurant, you'll need to use your Upromise-registered credit or debit cards. You must likewise use those cards when shopping at partner retailers or services. And you'll need to activate eCoupons to get even better offers at grocery stores.

Once you've earned $25, you can transfer the money to your 529 account—a smart idea, since money in the Upromise account doesn't earn interest, nor does it offer the tax advantages of a 529. You can also request a check to cover college expenses or link your Upromise and federal student loan accounts to pay down that debt.

Oh, and you can get your friends and family to help, too. Simply have them sign up their own store reward and credit cards and direct the contribution toward your account.

13 Rich, Successful People Who Went to State Schools

1. Oprah Winfrey. The queen of daytime, one of the most-well-known television personalities in history, attended Tennessee State University, where she had a full scholarship. She studied speech and drama and graduated in 1976. In 2013 she was worth $2.8 billion, according to *Forbes*.

2. Matt Groening. The creator of *The Simpsons* and *Futurama* attended a public liberal arts college in Olympia, Washington—Evergreen State University— where he studied philosophy.

3. Warren Buffett. His father insisted that Warren attend the University of Pennsylvania's Wharton School of Business as an undergraduate—but Buffett didn't think much of the quality of the education there. So he quickly transferred to the University of Nebraska-Lincoln. He worked full-time and graduated in three years. The head of wildly successful Berkshire Hathaway is now worth $53.5 billion, according to *Forbes*.

4. William McGuire. The longtime chief executive of United HealthCare graduated from University of Texas at Austin—which boasts a number of CEO graduates.

5. Gary Kelly. CEO and chairman of the board at everyone's favorite low-cost, fun-times airline, Southwest, graduated from UT-Austin with a degree in accounting and first joined Southwest as controller in 1986.

6. Donald Knauss. The chief executive of Clorox graduated from Indiana University. As of 2010, eight Fortune 500 CEOs were Indiana University grads, according to a compilation by *BusinessWeek* magazine.

7. David Novak. The chairman and chief executive of Yum! Brands—the company that brings you everything from Taco Bell to KFC to Pizza Hut—graduated from the University of Missouri with a bachelor's degree in journalism.

8. Rodger Riney. This Missouri graduate is founder and CEO of the highly successful deep-discount brokerage platform Scottrade, which aims to make investing more affordable for individuals.

9. and 10. Glenn Dubin and Henry Swieca. These childhood friends founded Highbridge Capital

Management, a $25-billion-dollar investment management firm that is now part of JPMorgan Chase & Co. They attended Stonybrook University, a New York public university.

11. Stephen King. One of the most prolific, popular, and successful novelists of all time went to the University of Maine, where he studied English and earned a teaching certificate.

12. David Tepper. The founder of hedge fund Appaloosa Management and widely known philanthropist graduated from the University of Pittsburgh in 1978 and worked his way through college. His net worth today: $7 billion, according to *Forbes*.

13. Beth Mooney. The only female CEO of a top 20 U.S. bank, Mooney graduated from University of Texas and could only find jobs as a bank secretary at first. Today she heads Cleveland-based $9 billion KeyCorp.

Who Knew?

5 Reasons State Schools May Be a Better Bet

. . . .

Private universities often offer better financial-aid packages than public colleges, and out-of-state tuition at top public universities can rival that of moderately priced private schools. But there are other reasons public universities can best private schools, and not just from a cost perspective.

1. Companies prefer to hire from them. A *Wall Street Journal* study found that when hiring for entry-level jobs, U.S. companies largely favor graduates of big state universities over Ivy League and other elite liberal arts schools. The study surveyed 479 companies, nonprofits, and government agencies that had collectively hired upward of 43,000 new graduates. They ranked state schools as top for hiring graduates for their education, work-readiness, and ability to succeed. Of the top 25 schools, only four were private, and just one Ivy League school—Cornell University—made the cut.

2. Public universities have a stronger career focus. Employers answering the *Wall Street Journal* survey often cited a need for new grads with practical skills to be operations managers, product developers, business analysts, and engineers—the bulk of their workforce.

State schools offer majors and classes relevant to specific types of jobs and often are better at preparing students for the actual work they may do after graduation, recruiters say.

3. They build corporate partnerships. Many state universities have master partnerships with big companies like DuPont, Lockheed Martin, Raytheon, and others, which give professors access to research. The companies often hire students as interns—and many go back to the schools to hire new graduates.

4. They try harder to attract the best and brightest. A number of state schools have scholarships—sometimes covering the bulk of the tuition costs—reserved for students at the very top of their high school graduating class. Others offer admission, with grants or tuition breaks, into specialized honors colleges and sweeten the financial deal for high schoolers being recruited by pricier private schools. These state schools may also work harder to attract big-name employers to recruit new grads and promote the school and its students to sought-after employers.

5. The CEO graduated from State U. Believe it or not, the majority of Fortune 500 CEOs attended state universities. And they are very loyal. John Brock, CEO of Coca-Cola and Georgia Institute of Technology graduate, told *The Wall Street Journal* that he always returned to his alma mater to recruit new hires, both while at Proctor & Gamble and as Coca-Cola CEO. Not long after Caterpillar Inc. opened new facilities in North Carolina, its CEO, North Carolina State University alum James Owens, "directed the company to step up recruiting from the school to fill the newly created jobs," he told the *Journal*.

And Macy's CEO Terry Lundgren opened a retailing center at his alma mater, Arizona State University, where he brings famous designers and retailers like Martha Stewart and Tommy Hilfiger to meet students and attend a global retail conference each year. This helps Arizona State retailing and marketing students get jobs that students at bigger-name, pricier colleges only dream of, with entry-level (or better) positions secured months before graduation. Carlos Moore, a 2010 graduate who studied graphic design, told *The Wall Street Journal* that after he was commissioned to film and photograph Lundgren during campus visits in 2009, Lundgren's assistant asked Moore to create a highlights DVD. That led to a marketing internship with Macy's in New York and a job offer after graduation. By fall 2010, Moore was working as a Macy's art director, creating layouts for Macy's publications.

5

Living Rich Without Going Broke

Your surroundings—the world, your office, your home—are all filled with things. Some of them are necessities, and many others are the makings of a rich life—those nice golf clubs, that high-quality cookware next to the fun kitchen gadgets, a backyard pool, postcards from that trip you took to Mexico.

Chances are, if you've been using your rich-guy vision, you didn't go overboard on them. But can you live richly without going broke, busting your budget, or skimping on savings?

Well, yes. Start by thinking about your definition of rich. Ray Dalio, founder of famously successful hedge fund Bridgewater Associates, was named one of the 50 richest people by *Forbes* magazine. And yet, he says living richly has almost nothing to do with money.

"Money is way overvalued because you can count it. If you could count happiness, if there were units and you asked, 'How many happiness points can I get?' and 'Could I put happiness points in the bank?'" says Dalio, who points to his family as the source of his life's richness, "we would live different lives because we would build up happiness points. That's what life is about."

Whatever brings you happiness doesn't have to cost a fortune. There are plenty of ways to travel, shop, eat out, and have fun without going broke.

13 Things Rich People Won't Tell You about Affording Luxury

1. Think it through. The wealthy know this concept all too well. You don't look before you leap; you don't do a business deal before you've really examined the books; you don't buy before you've thought about the implications. The same philosophy applies when it comes to buying a big-ticket item. Think through the value you will get and the amount of use you will get from the purchase. And make sure you have a plan in place to pay for your purchase—without jeopardizing your budget or your regular savings. If you've decided the purchase is worth it, be prepared to trim other expenses and divert some resources toward the newest item in your household.

2. Buy at the right time. How many stories have you read about one-time millionaires having to sell their

yacht or vacation home after the financial crisis?
Exactly. Because they are considered a luxury item,
boats are often the first possessions people—rich or
not—sell during a bad economy. "We bought our boat in
2009 from a very motivated seller who was looking to
liquidate and move from San Diego to a less expensive
city," says Erin Smith, who bought the cruiser with her
husband, Jenner. "She was selling it for less than it was
worth just a few months earlier in order to ensure a
quick sale."

**3. Spend the extra money on convenience if it
will enhance your luxury buy.** There's a reason the
wealthy belong to golf clubs or country clubs a short
drive from their homes. It's convenient—and they can
use the club almost like a second home, to entertain,
play tennis, have lunch. Joining the yacht club adds
an extra $400 to $500 per month to the cost of the

√ The **REAL** World

When Erin and Jenner Smith decided to buy a boat, their parents thought
they were nuts. The couple—Erin is editor of *San Diego* magazine, and
Jenner is a senior asset manager with the Port of San Diego—had just
spent most of their savings on a down payment for their first house, the
economy wasn't in great shape, they'd just adopted a puppy, and they
were trying to have a baby.

"We did it because we loved the idea, we both grew up on boats and
sailing in San Diego Bay, and we knew it was something we wanted to
do as a family together," says Erin. They found a great deal on a 25-foot
cruiser and joined a yacht club in San Diego.

boat, says Erin. But the convenience and the extra amenities—a pool, restaurant and bar, tennis courts, parking, and junior sailing program—make it worth the expense.

4. Consider the social benefit. Meeting other people who enjoy boating is a huge plus for Erin. "They understand both the expense and the joy that come from being a boat owner. And when we joined the club, we committed a good portion of our weekend social time to it," she says. And Diane Calloway, whose luxury purchase was a camper, says she and her family love inviting friends on their trips.

5. Make practical choices elsewhere in your discretionary spending. "We had the camper, but we couldn't afford to use it," says Diane. "So we decided to give up cable so we could afford to go camping. My husband is big into sports, but he said he could give it up." The couple also limited eating out to once a month, which Diane says makes those dinners out more special. And while their friends have upgraded to bigger or newer campers, Diane and her husband have kept their simple camper because "there's no reason to buy something more. It's easy to pinch pennies when there's a payoff," she says.

6. Don't bother with other status symbols. Erin and Jenner knew that a car can be a status symbol, especially in California. "But when we decided to get a boat, we consciously chose to scale back the amount

√ The **REAL** World

Diane Calloway and her husband, Brian, grew up camping and can't imagine not camping dozens of times a year with friends. Until they had their first daughter five years ago, they camped in a tent. Now they own a modest camper that Diane says she negotiated a good deal on—even though they were pinching pennies to build their first house at the same time. The couple, both engineers, work during the week and focus their weekends on spending time with their daughters. And that means lots and lots of camping trips.

of money and importance we put towards our cars," Erin says. At first they scaled back to one car and one motor scooter and decided to buy used, delaying their second car purchase until they could amass a big down payment and bargain for a low interest rate. After just three years of owning the boat, they now also own two cars, one paid for and the other to be paid off in the next year—both 2004 Toyotas.

7. A penny saved is a headache spared. After the first year of owning their boat, the couple knew what the annual maintenance cost would be and set up an automatic savings plan to pay for it. "In a similar way that we save for property taxes and retirement, we have a certain amount of money that automatically goes into a savings account for the boat each month before we even see it. That way, the $1,000 maintenance that we need for the boat each year doesn't become a stressful expense," says Erin.

8. Use that luxury. Many people already in the millionaires club belong to a country club, a golf club, and sometimes a yacht or tennis club, and they use the facilities as often as possible. Diane and Brian and Erin and Jenner have something in common: They get a lot of use out of their "luxury purchase." By doing so, they get a lot of return on their investment—and they often aren't spending extra money elsewhere. "When some people are spending $100 out at dinner and a movie on the weekends, we are sharing wine with friends on the boat or swimming with the kids at the club's pool," says Erin. As for Diane and her family, "We have a camping trip booked every two weeks for most of the year through August."

9. Negotiate, negotiate. Diane says she bargained down the price of the camper—and has done the same for almost everything she buys—by doing her homework and coming to the table with facts about what the item should cost, what others have paid recently, and even the specs that make one product less valuable (or more) than another.

10. Play one vendor off another. As part of her overall saving-smart strategy, Diane went back and forth between Sears and Lowe's over the price of appliances for their new home, built in 2010. Diane knew she wanted stainless steel, and she knew she wanted one of the pricier refrigerators on the market—a French-door stainless with a freezer pull-out on the bottom. The set they wanted was more than they'd normally spend, a luxury. "We started out at Lowe's and found what we liked, walked over to Sears and got a quote, and then we went back to Lowe's and asked for their best deal," says Diane.

11. Know the inside code. But that negotiation didn't end there for Diane. She discovered that if you plan to buy a lot of merchandise from Lowe's, you can get a discount. She and her husband went through the store and made a list of everything they could possibly need for their new home, from light fixtures to trash cans to sink mountings—and yes, those fancy appliances. They asked for the discount—something most people except contractors know to ask for—and the store manager sent the list to corporate headquarters to calculate a possible discount, which is based on the number of items that you say you'll buy. The couple got 17 percent off everything they purchased at Lowe's. And Diane got her French-door fridge for less than even Sears' price.

12. Higher deductibles mean more money in your pocket. Look for other places to trim without "depriving" yourself. You can save substantially, for example, by increasing the deductibles on the comprehensive and collision portions of your auto insurance policy. According to the Insurance Information Institute, raising collision deductibles from $200 to $500 could reduce your collision and comprehensive coverage costs by 15 to 30 percent. Squeeze out additional savings by asking about every possible discount, such as for carpooling, air bags, annual mileage below 10,000 miles—even for teenage drivers with grade averages above a B.

13. Switch from pay to free. If you've been spending $15 a month on Netflix or $20 a month for On Demand movies, consider cutting the wireless cord, so to speak. Check out movies from your local library, where the cost is zilch. Spending less on one form of entertainment means you can spend more on your luxury buy. That $20 buys several gallons of gas for that boat or camper, or whatever your luxe purchase is.

Bouncing Back

Shop Savvy—Make That Free . . .

....

Kathy Spencer, founder of HowToShopForFree.net and coauthor, with Samantha Rose, of the book *How to Shop for Free: Shopping Secrets for Smart Woman Who Love to Get Something for Nothing,* is a lifelong bargain-hunter.

She grew up in a low-income area, learned to clip coupons from her mom, and scored her first find as a teenager—a pair of then-trendy Jordache jeans for $4 at Marshalls. She started "extreme couponing" six years ago, when pneumonia left her husband, the family's primary earner, unable to work and the bills started to pile up. The 42-year-old mother of four and former loan officer for a mortgage company says she's saved hundreds of thousands of dollars by knowing what she wants and then doing the work to find it for less, or even for free.

"People can have anything they want if they stick to it and find deals," she says. "I'm living proof."

Spencer and her family live in a 3,000-square-foot home in affluent Boxford, Massachusetts. She says it's all about appearances—looking like they're keeping up with the Joneses by being smarter than the Joneses.

"People come to the house and think we have it made," she says. They have the latest tech toys—touch-screen computer and tablets—a pricey Dyson vacuum (these retail for upward of $300) and a big flat-screen television. The family wears designer clothes—Spencer says Abercrombie is actually cheaper than Kmart when purchased just before the next season's line comes into stores. That's when there are markdowns upon markdowns on merchandise. Spencer and her family have paid for their cars in cash and carry no credit card debt.

How can you score the same kind of savings? Read on for Kathy's strategies.

13 Things the Wannabe Rich Know about Shopping on a Regular Gal Budget

1. Deals, deals, and more deals. Kathy Spencer uses coupons and rebates and stacks store promotions—that is, a sale plus store coupons plus special offers—to buy almost everything.

2. Buy and sell. When Spencer finds a hot item that she really wants, she first checks online-auction-site eBay to see if it's hard to find—in this case, a much-coveted Wii. She did a little reconnaissance to see where to buy the Wii locally—and what time the delivery truck would arrive. She showed up early to score one. Later that day, she sold it on eBay at a $70 profit, which she used to buy a Wii for her family at a discounted price. Depending on the item, Spencer has purchased a few at a time, selling all but one on eBay, using the profits to cover the cost of the product she keeps.

3. There's no shame in paying less. Don't fret over the "status" that prices can convey, especially if you're living in an affluent area. Find what you want on a clearance rack, rip off the sale tag after you get the item home, and remember that you've spent smarter than your more status-conscious pals.

4. Be willing to do a little bit of work to live fashionably frugal. Focus on what you want—a new dishwasher or trendy jeans—and then do the work to find a bargain or free money. States offer high-value Energy Star rebates on energy-efficient appliances right around Earth Day—the same time when stores often put those appliances on sale. Spencer purchased a hybrid water heater on sale for $1,000—and got a $1,000 rebate. *Voilà*, free water heater.

5. Get your daily deal on. Spencer, like many others these days, uses daily deal sites like Groupon and LivingSocial, which offer discounts on local restaurants, shops, and services, plus rewards for referring additional customers. She recently used a LivingSocial voucher to get a car starter installed for free—she paid $129 for the voucher, then posted the deal on her Facebook page. Within an hour three friends snapped it up—which meant she got the deal for free, saving $129. "Everyone knows three people who'd go to a restaurant and would appreciate the deal," she says, but most people are too lazy to go the extra step for an even better deal.

6. Buy junk, buy it twice. Know what you're buying by doing the research and reading all the product reviews you can find—and pay particular attention to those on the most-trusted websites. Spencer bought three name-brand stainless-steel kitchen appliances at a special three-for-one price, but neither read product reviews nor did enough research—and eventually had to replace them all. Had she done her homework, she says she is "pretty confident I would not have ever purchased that brand."

7. Shop till you profit. There are a number of shopping sites—eBates.com, RetailMeNot.com, and MrRebates.com, among others—that offer both coupons and rebates for shopping at specific stores. Spencer uses ebates.com. She looks for the product she wants, buys it online using one of the site's coupons, but she chooses to pick up the item at the store itself. And four times a year she gets a check for the accumulated rebates.

8. Borrow that bag or dress—or rent it. There are at least four websites that, for a fee, allow you to rent a designer bag, dress, or accessory. Among them: BagBorrowSteal.com, RentTheRunway.com, and LendingLuxury.com. Some offer insurance (in case you spill on a fancy dress or tear a Louis Vuitton bag) for a fee, and some offer insurance and return shipping free of charge. You may need to sign up for a (free) membership or be invited to join. In addition, search your local area for luxury rental shops—you'd be surprised how many bricks-and-mortar options there may be. Bottom line: When you want a taste of the luxe fashion life, why spend $800 on a dress when you can rent it for $75 for a week?

9. Get Gilt. The website, that is, or RueLaLa.com or ShopItToMe.com. These sites offer luxury items, from fashion to home goods to travel and more, for as much as 70 percent off retail prices. You do have to act quickly, as they often hold flash sales or have limited quantities of merchandise to offer.

10. Become a Maxxinista or a HomeGoods loyalist. Shopping at an off-pricer is like a game of hide-and-seek. Find out when the store receives shipments. Great deals go fast, so be prepared to spend some time going through racks and bins searching for a good deal.

11. Sign up for coupons from designer stores and high-end outlets. Yes, you may end up with a lot of e-mail junk mail and some coupons you won't use. But many high-end outlets, like Off Fifth (Saks Fifth Avenue's outlet) and Last Call by NM (Neiman Marcus), carry first-rate merchandise, not second-rate merchandise designed with cheaper fabric or less-sturdy stitching just for the outlets. It might be last year's style, but when you get a 40-percent-off coupon for email list customers and hit a holiday weekend sale, you can snag an already discounted item for rock-bottom prices. How about a Nicole Miller work dress for $60? That's what Susan from suburban New York paid for a dress whose original retail price was $430. The discount price at Off Fifth was $200—plus half-off clearance sale and a 40-percent-off coupon.

12. Work the retail cycle. Nicole Russo, a New York City style consultant, writes on her shopping blog: "Assuming you live in a four-season climate, inventory arrives in stores two to four months before you would actually be able to wear the clothes. For example, summer clothes come in now when it's 49 degrees. Shop later in the retail season (when you'd actually wear the stuff) and you'll save money, because many pieces will be marked down. Almost everything goes on sale. Wait it out if you can—just keep a close eye on your size."

13. High-end consignment is your friend. Where do the wealthy dump their clothes, unwanted furniture, and Jimmy Choo shoes? That's right, consignment stores. At least some of them do. Those items are then resold for a fraction of the price. Buy designer consignment and, yes, do the reverse. When you're ready to part with your finds, take them to consignment, too. Shops will pay you up to 50 percent of the final sale price or give you store credit of even more so you can restock your own shelves. The same goes for church or charity-group furniture stores in ritzy neighborhoods. Cast-off leather couches, four-poster beds, and Victorian-era bureaus can be had for pennies on the (original) dollar.

13 Things Rich People Won't Tell You about Negotiating a Good Deal for a Car

1. Ask the questions others typically don't ask. Chief among them: How long has this car been on your lot? Every day a car sits on a dealer's lot, it costs them in insurance premiums. Ask which cars have been on the lot the longest—they are likely more eager to get rid of those first and will cut a better deal. Whether it's a Bentley or a Toyota, it's a good way to score a discount.

2. The best time to buy is at the end of the month. Ever wonder why so many business deals close at the end of the month? To get in under the wire for monthly reports or quarterly earnings. The end of the month is also when dealers need to fill their quotas. Or better still, at the end of each quarter (March, June, September,

December), says Gary Foreman of stretcher.com. Negotiate up from the invoice price (what the dealer paid for the car, easy to find on the Web), not down from the sticker price.

3. Never negotiate empty-minded. Look at price comparison websites like edmunds.com to find out what people are paying at dealers near you. Also check out kbb.com (Kelley Blue Book) to research makes and models. Cars.com will send your request to dealers for competitive quotes.

4. Determine the real cost to own. Know how much it costs to run a vehicle over five to eight years. You can use the True Cost to Own tool at edmunds.com to compare makes and models. You might find that a car that costs $3,000 less upfront will cost double that savings in maintenance and gas over five years.

5. Tell them you've secured financing elsewhere. The dealerships will almost always counteroffer, and you'll go with the best deal. It's something wealthy buyers, if they don't buy in cash, do regularly since they can often secure better deals at private banks. You can, too, usually by contacting local credit unions.

6. You'll pay for that guaranteed trade-in price. Ever wonder about those ads that promise a minimum $3,000 trade-in value for your clunker? Those dealerships also pad the sales price to make up for the difference.

7. Don't give away all your cards. It's a negotiation tactic that the wealthy have used in everything from sealing a deal to, yes, buying a car or getting a better deal at a bank. Did you have an accident in your last car and now you really need a pair of wheels? Is your old car on its last fume? Don't tell the car dealer. Once the salesperson knows your weakness, you lose your negotiating power.

8. If you can't walk away, don't come to the table. Be prepared to walk away if you can't get to a price or terms that you agree on—it's practically the mantra that has saved many a rich guy from a bad financial decision. Since you will walk in the door with a price and options in mind, if you don't get all or close to what you asked for, walk away. It might feel painful and you might have just wasted three hours of time, but you may just end up with a better deal. Plus, car dealers and negotiation experts say this tactic is one in the repertoire of the wealthy—and it's one reason they get better deals when they buy cars (even if their price point is thousands, or tens of thousands, of dollars higher than yours).

9. Never pay the VIN-etch fee. It's a $250 optional add-on that's almost pure profit for car dealers. And you don't really need it.

10. Never sign tired. Worn out and ready to go home, you sign document after document. Then you wake up the next day, look down, and you signed a contract with a $1,995 extended warranty that isn't worth the paper it's written on. And you're stuck.

11. Sure, I'd be happy to do that—for a price. A dealer will tint your windows, apply rustproofing, or paint a pinstripe on your truck. But they'll probably charge you two or three times the cost of doing it elsewhere. Research after-market services to find a better deal.

12. Ask for a full tank of gas. A new-car salesman will usually give you a tank of gas when you drive off the lot. But used-car dealers don't often do the same— unless you ask. Consider that, say, for a truck or large SUV, that tank of gas might cost nearly $100. But for the sales guy, a tank of gas is an easier give than another $100 off the price of the car.

13. Do not buy the extended-service warranty. The manufacturer warranty you get when you purchase or lease your car is legit. The one you're offered via a postcard in the mail, in all likelihood, is not. According to an investigation by the Better Business Bureau of St. Louis—home to several warranty companies—nearly $3 million in repairs that should have been covered according to contracts weren't. What's more, over 90 percent of those who purchased such insurance found the process to be "misleading or improper."

Great Advice

8 Ways to Stay Fit and Mind Your Health on a Dime

You've been saving, spending smart, and looking forward to the rich life ahead. But you'll have to take care of yourself to really enjoy it and live as richly as you want to. Many fitness options are free—a walk, a hike, running with a friend. But if you're going to spend a little, spend smart.

Blythe Burton-Teed, a naturopathic doctor, says people end up spending lots of money on medications that they could easily be taken off of if they changed their lifestyle a little bit. "The majority of my patients can come off of hypertensive medications or diabetes medications within the first weeks" of changing their lifestyle, says Burton-Teed.

"It can be a difficult transition for people, especially when it seems like you have to spend more money to join the gym or buy workout gear or pay for a weight-loss program," says Burton-Teed. "But in the long run—and in the short run for all of the other benefits—investing in your health in the right way makes a lot of financial sense."

Here are some tips from pros and regular Joes and Janes about how to stay fit and healthy without spending a lot. Of course, talk with your doctor before you start any fitness or diet program.

1. Try a dental college. Beatrice, a Maryland twenty-something, had her wisdom teeth removed through a dental college to save money. She had dental insurance, but her co-pay was so high, she decided to search for a discount. A nearby dental college offered services by students just about to graduate—under the supervision of an experienced dentist—and Beatrice saved hundreds of dollars.

2. Or any college, for that matter. The same deals can be had at colleges and training programs for aesthesticians, hairdressers, and even massage therapists or acupuncturists. Nicole, from Baltimore, says she got free acupuncture when she went to the Tai Sophia Institute for acupuncture. The service—to help her alleviate headaches—was provided by a student finishing her last-year clinical requirements. "Everything was supervised by licensed acupuncturists," Nicole says. Massage students also have to log a certain number of hours in order to get their license and often offer deep discounts to achieve those goals.

3. Play discount-class-roulette. Beatrice also takes advantage of discount deals for health classes. She'll buy a month of unlimited cross-fit classes one month, Zumba classes another month, kickboxing another month. Since these discounts are usually only good for first-time class attendees, she rotates her classes and supplements by buying discounted drop-in class cards. Sometimes the month of classes can be had for as little as $30, particularly at new exercise studios or when a gym offers a new class and is trying to build up attendance. Discounts can also be found on Groupon and LivingSocial.

4. It pays to try something new. Nicole says that while scouting around for acupuncture deals, she also started trying different massage therapists via discount first-time user coupons or deals. At one that was recommended to her, she scored three massages for less than the price of two and found a massage therapist she really liked. Nicole came in with a voucher that gave her a 60-minute massage for $35, a $40 savings. New customers who came in through the vouchers get a $15 discount every time they come back. Now Nicole gets $75 massages for just $60 and gets a free 30-minute massage for every person she refers.

5. Volunteer or work a few hours in a gym to get a free membership. Local recreation centers and sometimes YMCAs look for volunteers or workers who just want a few hours per week. In exchange, they often also offer a free membership and deeply discounted memberships for family members, which can save hundreds of dollars per year.

6. Go local. Your employer may provide gym discounts or reimbursements. Take advantage (and watch the reimbursement filing deadlines). Some homeowner's associations offer discounted yoga or other fitness classes in the community clubhouse. Many local parks, recreation departments, and even churches offer free or inexpensive fitness centers or weekly programs. Why pay $15 per yoga class when, say, you could pay $8 or $10 by going to church to exercise?

7. Go big, but get more. In areas where a fancy health club is available, the cost of a monthly membership for the family could be more than $125. But before you balk, consider this: If, say, the club offers free babysitting while you work out, discounted or free programs for children, a swimming pool, and all the classes you'd normally have to pay are included in the monthly cost, it might end up saving you money. Write down what other expenses you could cut by joining, and compare the cost of the membership and the savings to decide.

8. Prescription drugs for less. You've probably heard that Wal-Mart sells a 30-day supply of more than 300 drugs (mostly generics) for just $4 per order. So do Giant Eagle, Kroger Pharmacy, and Target. Wal-Mart, Kroger, Target, and Kmart sell a 90-day supply for $10. Based on the experiences of more than 40,000 *Consumer Reports* readers, Costco is the cheapest source. And you don't have to pay Costco's annual membership fee to use its pharmacy. You can get prescriptions filled both in store and online. In most cases it costs far less to get 3-month supplies of medications you take regularly.

13 Ways to Travel Rich—Even Abroad—without Breaking the Bank

1. Tag along with a traveling spouse. The wealthy tend to travel a lot, largely for business. And sometimes those business meetings and conferences are held in fabulous locales, like Paris or Prague or—closer to home—San Francisco or New York City. It's not uncommon for a spouse to tag along and make a weekend of it after the business is done. But you don't have to be rich to do the same. Vicki Bringman tagged along on many trips with her now-retired husband, Lew. A trip to Seattle, for instance, for a work conference meant Vicki spent two days exploring Seattle and then she and Lew paid for the extra nights they stayed in the conference hotel. "My hotel is covered [during the conference], and I often traveled on his frequent-flier miles," says Vicki. "So all we're paying is extra lodging and for activities and meals."

2. Remember, a hotel is where you sleep—spend accordingly. Bringman says she only has three criteria for a hotel: It has to be clean, it has to be convenient, and it has to be safe. Usually that means finding a hotel in a decent neighborhood that's close to transportation and isn't, well, gross. "Anything else, I can live with," says Bringman. "I don't need the luxurious first-class hotel—you spend so few hours in a hotel room that it just seems senseless to spend so much on a hotel room." Those hotel savings, she says, have allowed her to spend more on experiences while abroad and help make traveling more affordable overall.

3. Rent an apartment instead—through an owner, if possible. There are usually thousands of apartments available through various websites that specialize in tourist rentals. Browse them and consider whether having a kitchen to cook a few meals in and store food will stretch your travel dollars. It almost always will if you plan to travel for a week or more—the usual minimum for an apartment rental. Try to find an apartment that's in a residential district within the city so you can get a real flavor for the lifestyle and culture of a place. Some apartments, if you search, are offered by owner—an even cheaper option because you don't have an agency fee to pay.

4. Talk to a human, not the website. Seth Kugel, former Frugal Traveler blogger for *The New York Times*, told *Reader's Digest* this trick: "I called a place in Barbados. It was the off-season, and I said, 'Is that your cheapest room? What if I stayed a few extra days?' She said, 'Well, I can offer you the rate for Caribbean citizens.' Caricom is the term for the Caribbean community, and there's a rate for native Caribbeans. It was really easy for her, and it would never have come up online. Only by my calling the hotel did she think of saying, 'Oh, we can slip you in under this Caricom rate.'"

> **$ TOP SECRET!** Eat out at lunchtime. Lunch menus often offer the same dishes as in the evening for a sizeable discount. Have your main meal at lunch, or get the cheaper lunchtime specials to go and save them for dinner.

5. Book far, far in advance—or at the very last minute. The further out you book, the more likely you are to get best-priced airfare and even some hotel discounts. How many times have you planned a trip somewhere but waited to buy your tickets, only to read about an airfare hike? Exactly. Of course, the alternative—if you have a flexible life—is to wait until the last minute. Most airlines have last-minute deal e-newsletters that go out midweek for travel over the next weekend. They're eager to sell seats on half-full planes, and you can score some excellent deals on airfare and sometimes companion hotel deals, too.

6. Don't always follow the tourist guidebooks for food advice. First off, they tend to be pricier. Second, they tend to be crowded. And third, they tend to be Americanized versions of local foods. Instead, follow your nose—or follow the locals by asking for advice— to smaller establishments with true local cuisine and,

$ TOP SECRET! If you're shopping for a flight on the Web and the flight prices keep going up, not down, trash your cookies! Many sites install cookies on your computer when you visit—a collection of information that will include your username and the date and time you visited the site. Sometimes travel websites use this information to increase their prices if you repeatedly run the same searches for airlines or hotels. Before you buy a ticket, erase the cookies from your computer.

often, lower prices meant to appeal to locals. Just be sure you know the names of the foods you don't like in the native language in case there's no English translation on the menu. In most non-tourist restaurants, there won't be.

7. Eat out less, picnic more. Bringman and her husband have gone to Paris every January for the last seven years to celebrate her birthday. They've also traveled extensively through Europe and the United States, and everywhere they go, they picnic. In France they may grab cheese from a local grocery store, bread from a bakery, and sit down on a bench or roll out a small blanket in a park and watch the world around them while they eat. *Voilà!* Lunch for a few dollars, more money to spend on a nice dinner or souvenirs—and a rich experience of watching the pace and life of the city around you.

8. Skip the airport taxi. The airport may be 20 miles or more from a city center, and a taxi can cost $50 to $75. But a train, shuttle bus, or public bus could cost just $10 to $15. For instance, a taxi from Charles de Gaulle airport outside Paris to the center of the city costs the equivalent of $60. But a train or bus will cost about $10. Yes, you'll have to lug your bags twice—once on the way, once on the way back. But it will be worth it when you save that extra $50 for a nice dinner out or a trip to a cultural landmark.

9. Scout out museum and city sightseeing passes. Most cities in the United States and abroad with several museums or cultural landmarks will offer a discounted pass to get into a number of these locations for a fee that can be half the cost of paying for each one individually. Just be aware of expiration dates—some require that you use the passes consecutive days; others allow you a week's worth of entry. Before you leave home, research the best deals online and find out when the museums or landmarks you want to see offer free entry. You may be able to schedule your days to get into your choice locales for free and save even more.

10. Travel off-season or midweek, and not just to save money. Of course, discounts abound during the less-popular off-seasons and shoulder seasons. Says Kugel: "Huge tourist destinations are the best bet for sharp discounts in the off-season because these economies are completely dependent on tourist income as opposed to business-travel income." But there's another good reason to travel when others are staying home: crowds. You can get far more enjoyment out of a trip—and feel you're living rich without breaking the bank—by visiting popular destinations during slow times. Bringman and her husband, for instance, travel a lot in the off-season. It's cheaper to fly, she says, and "I prefer to travel off-season when you don't have a city full of tourists, and the weather is better than the heat of summer."

11. Shop flea, especially abroad. Paris is famous for its out-of-the-way flea markets, where leather jackets can be had for half the cost of what you'd pay in the United States, and you never know what deals you'll find. Most major tourist cities have flea markets with local goods and artisan wares. Ask locals for advice on where to find flea markets, antique markets, and even quiet side streets with unique boutiques that aren't always advertised. Bringman, for instance, found a $20 Italian-made suede purse in a small shop on a side street. A number of U.S. cities also have such markets. As for the main shopping avenues—pick up an inexpensive souvenir there to say you've been, but nothing more.

12. Shop the (private) discount travel sites. There are so many discount travel websites to choose from. Which should you consider? Of course, the usual, like Kayak.com, are in order, but also consider private sale sights. They are member-only—but it's usually not hard to become a member by searching online for an invite code, and it's usually free. Check out these sites— and compare them to the deals you've found on your own: Jetsetter.com, SniqueAway.com, TripAlertz.com. TabletHotels.com, and Vacationist.com. Often you'll find a better deal on the private sale site, but your dates may need to be flexible.

BECOME AN INSTANT EXPERT
6 Restaurant Apps and Deal Websites to Save Big Bucks Eating Out

Savored.com, for discreet cheap dates. You can make free reservations for dinner at your city's premiere hot spots for up to 40 percent off a meal (and for once, booze included!) and through their software, the discount is automatically factored into your final tab so you can dine in discounts (and style) discreetly.

BlackboardEats.com, for gourmet bargains. Score up to 30 percent off meals at restaurants throughout Los Angeles, New York, San Francisco, and Chicago. The app allows you to read restaurant reviews and purchase your favorite deals on the fly.

Scoutmob.com, for the regulars. Browse Return Perk deals that offer 10 to 50 percent off meals, with extra savings for regulars at restaurants in Austin, Boston, Washington, and other cities. You have to be at the location to access the deal.

KidsEatFor.com, for deal-happy parents. When you've got children and want to dine out, KidsEatFor.com finds local restaurants where kids eat for free or a large discount.

OpenTable.com, for social rewards. Make a reservation and message friends with a time, date, and location to earn Dining Rewards Points that you can redeem for discounts.

Restaurant.com, to get more for less. You can browse discounts in your area. Pay $10 for a $25 certificate, select a restaurant, then print out the dining certificate and present it to your waiter. Be sure to read the fine print for restrictions first; some restaurants don't allow the certificates to be used on weekends or holidays, and most require a minimum food purchase of $10 to $15 more than the certificate's value. But, even if you spend $40 eating out, your real total is a much lower $25 after the discount certificate is applied. A number of restaurants also offer $15 certificates for $6—great for a lunch out with friends. If your company offers a rewards program with Restaurant.com, you'll occasionally be offered those $25 certificates for just $4, turning that $40 meal into a $19 one.

💰 TOP SECRET! **Sit at the bar during happy hour at a nice restaurant. Often, the menu will be virtually the same as if you sit at a table, but you may get half-price appetizers and, sometimes, half-price meals during certain hours.**

13. Use travel-pro tools.

The website itasoftware.com is used by travel agents, travel websites, and the airlines themselves. Although you can't book your tickets through this site, it does offer lots of other benefits. You're allowed to choose where you fly from and where you're flying to, just like the other sites, but you can also search airports up to 300 miles away from your destinations. In addition, you can see available flights on the days before or after your target dates. Once you find the flights you need, click the "details" icon, which then gives you the flight numbers, booking codes, and fare codes for each flight on your itinerary. At this point, you simply call a travel agent—or call the airlines directly—with the information.

Great Advice

5 Reasons to Consider a House Swap

· ·

If you're a budget-conscious traveler looking for something more than the typical hotel experience on your next vacation, house swapping may be for you. Here's why:

1. It's inexpensive. It goes without saying that affordability is what first attracts most house swappers. Subtracting the cost of accommodations from a travel budget can make visiting a dream destination a reality.

2. You'll feel at home away from home. Staying in a hotel is a nice escape, but it gives you a very different perspective on a place than actually living among the locals. Unlike rentals, house swaps often take place in an owner's year-round residence and can include the use of their car and even the care of their pets (if you agree). Nothing makes you feel like one of the neighbors than stopping by the local café for coffee and the paper while taking "your" dog for a walk at 7:00 A.M.

3. It's great for kids. Just packing to travel with kids can leave you feeling like you need a vacation. Swapping homes with a family, however, means you can leave the Pack 'n' Play, stroller, and giant bag of Legos at home. The key is to find a family with kids similar in age to your own so that their bikes, toys, books, and DVDs will be well matched for your brood.

4. It slows you down—in a good way. Too often, traveling abroad means trying to take in an entire country—or continent—in one trip. A house swap is the polar opposite of those seven-cities-in-seven-days whirlwind tours. Staying put for a week or two affords you the luxury of really getting to know a place and allows you to enjoy some downtime without feeling like you should be on your way to the next major attraction.

5. You'll eat—and shop—like a local. Having a kitchen doesn't mean you'll eat in every night, but it does give you the option of whipping up a light meal after a long day of sightseeing. And if the culinary inspiration strikes, you may end up creating some of your best memories shopping in local markets and re-creating regional specialties in "your" kitchen.

Three popular home-exchange websites are HomeExchange.com, HomeLink.org, Domuswap.com.

Who Knew?
Get First-Class Treatment in Coach

· ·

These days, nearly every major airline will offer you extra legroom or entrance to their VIP lounge—if you're willing to pay for it. As part of a growing trend, some airlines have begun offering economy passengers the option to purchase comprehensive packages of perks once reserved for first- and business-class travelers. Here's a shortlist:

American Airlines Five Star Service Program. One hundred and twenty-five dollars gets you (or you and your spouse, for $200) the full VIP experience on American—at least until you board the plane. Choose from three service options: departure assistance, connection assistance, or arrival assistance. Each option provides you with a personal assistant to handle everything from booking a car service to checking you in to expediting security. Once you're near the gate, relax in the Admirals Club lounge while your assistant coordinates any last-minute requests with the in-flight crew before finally ushering you onto the plane—ahead of the queue.

JetBlue Even More Space (with Even More Speed). Offered on select flights, Even More Space lets you book seats with extra legroom for an additional fee (ranging from $10 to $75 per flight leg), depending on the destination. In several cities an additional perk known as Even More Speed—which gets you through security and boarding faster—is offered along with Even More Space— though it's not available separately.

United Premier. United offers both a la carte or combo platter options for its VIP services. Choose from expedited security and boarding (Premier Line, from $9), hassle-free baggage (Door-to-Door Baggage, $79; Luggage Free/Luggage Forward, from $225), or extra legroom (Economy Plus, from $9), or one of the packages, including several options (Premier Seating, from $65; Premier Travel, from $47). Brand-loyal frequent travelers can even pay for a full year of baggage for a flat rate of $349 through United's Premier Baggage program.

Delta Economy Comfort & Preferred Seats. Priority boarding, extra legroom, free alcoholic drinks, and super-reclining seats are all included in Delta's VIP offering, which is available only on international flights. Prices range from $80 to $160 per flight leg and vary according to ticket fare. Domestic travelers who are members of Delta's SkyMiles program can request the best seats in the house (or, in this case, plane) through the Preferred Seating option. SkyMiles members are also eligible for Priority Waitlist Status for upgrades once they've purchased a ticket.

Great Advice

5 Luxuries and Extras Not Worth the Money

....

1. Credit card payment insurance. For a monthly fee, many credit card companies offer an optional insurance policy: They'll cover your payments if you become disabled or unemployed. Financial advisers say that most of these programs are rife with complex rules and restrictions and recommend using the money you would have spent on insurance to pay down your balance instead.

2. Unlimited cell phone minutes. You may think you need a cell phone plan with unlimited minutes so you have the freedom to talk as much as you like without incurring extra fees. But most people don't exceed the number of minutes offered in even the least expensive plans from most carriers (about 700 per month for a family plan). Check your usage amount on bills for the past several months before making a decision.

3. Bottled water. Contrary to what most bottled-water producers would like you to think, much of what they're bottling comes straight from a tap rather than a spring or well. Using a water filter will give you similar results for a fraction of the price. It's also kinder to the planet—most plastic water bottles end up in landfills rather than at recycling facilities.

4. Group tours in foreign locales. Outside of a basic bus tour to get a lay of the land, paying for excursions is usually a waste of money. You can almost always plan the same trip to a landmark or town on the outskirts in a foreign city for far less, traveling by train and buying discount tickets ahead of time, say travel pros.

5. Long-distance calls. Skype's website says it all: "Make calls from your computer—free to other people on Skype and cheap to landlines and cell phones around the world." You'll need a computer headset or a microphone and speakers. You can even make free video calls with a webcam. Download free software (in 28 languages) at skype.com.

6

Retire Smart

Ah, retirement. The golden years of traveling, doing the things you never had time to do when you were raising children and climbing the career ladder. You've got big plans. Sell the house, move south—close to a beach or a golf course—and live out your days on the fairway, with trips to see the grandkids, the Grand Canyon, and maybe the Seven Wonders of the World.

Most people tend to think only of the here and now, and planning beyond those active finally-doing-what-I-want years can be difficult when it's hard to even imagine not wanting to play nine holes or take that next eight-day trip.

According to Michael Kay, a registered investment adviser in Livingston, New Jersey, and president of advisory firm Financial Focus, to live richly, it's crucial to plan for the three stages of retirement: The go-go years, when you're at your most vibrant and active; the slow-go years, when your health may start to deteriorate and you'd rather stay home than travel; and the no-go years, when you rely on others to help navigate your life.

13 Things Rich People Won't Tell You about Planning a More Secure Retirement

1. Think about what matters most. Develop both a life and financial strategy for each stage of your retirement, starting with the question: What do I value the most? Think about what's most important to you—and then build a financial plan with an adviser starting with those musts. "People may talk about buying the beach house or lavish vacations. But what they really, really want is to be able to have that sense of security," says investment adviser Michael Kay. "Regardless of whether they are very wealthy or middle class, they want the same things—they want to put their head on the pillow at night and feel secure they aren't going to run out of money."

2. Set your mind to it. Think about what you want to do each day during those go-go retirement years, and start by asking yourself if there was, at an earlier stage of your life, anything you wanted to do or be. If you plan to do that in retirement, envision how that daily routine would look. And consider what your plan would be if you couldn't, say, play tennis every day.

3. Take a good look at your health. Look at both your current health and your history. Are there any challenges or obstacles, and are they immediate or down the road? Also consider that in 20 years you may need a whole lot more money to pay increased costs of health care—and have more health-care needs.

4. Open the door to new experiences. Think about activities that would be interesting to explore. Prioritize them by considering what you really want to do and likely will do. And consider how you can use your skills and abilities to benefit others in a way that would be gratifying to you.

5. Your house doesn't always have to be your home. Why do you want to change, and where do you want to live? Will that location be a help or hindrance to the other things you want to do? What's most important to you about where you live?

6. Look back and learn. Think back to your most successful transition—say, from a line manager to head of the department, or from a single guy to a married man. Think about how you managed the change and how you can take that great experience and apply it to your transition from 9 to 5 to retirement.

7. Assess your assets. Generally, you'll have three possible asset "buckets" to draw on in retirement. Investments—your 401(k), Individual Retirement Account, cash-value life insurance, and other investment accounts; Social Security benefits; and, if you're lucky, a pension. What to draw on when? Now's the time to seek financial advice.

> **$ TOP SECRET!** A worker entitled to $1,000 per month in Social Security benefits at age 66 would get 25 percent less, or $750 per month, if he signed up at age 62. If he waited until age 70 to collect, he would get $1,320 a month, 32 percent more, according to a *U.S. News & World Report* analysis. There is no additional benefit for waiting beyond age 70.

8. Now's the time for that adviser. The years approaching retirement are the time when you'll most need financial advice. A financial adviser or planner will help you prioritize pools of money for drawing down now and saving for later when your health-care costs or financial needs for care might be much higher.

9. Reconsider your aversion to risk. To make your income sources last through the slow-go and expensive no-go phases, you may need to keep a portion of your investments in a portfolio that seems more suitable for someone 20 years younger—like stocks and stock

Become an Instant Expert
What to Expect When You're Expecting to Retire

There are three phases of retirement; how long each phase lasts depends partly on your health and personal circumstances. "No one is going to come around with a sign saying YOU ARE NOW ENTERING THE NEXT STAGE," says Kay. "While you are cognizant and fully aware as you approach retirement, this is the time to think about it [and] prepare for these next stages."

Here's what to expect:

The go-go years: The years when you are at your most vibrant and most active. You may travel, be involved in organizations, nonprofits, and even part-time or consulting work. You'll have the energy and desire to do the fun things you put off until retirement. The world is your oyster.

The slow-go years: Your health may start to deteriorate a bit, with illnesses lingering. You might prefer to stay home rather than take that next trip. "When the idea of going to an airport for any reason just becomes miserable, you are in or near the slow-go stage," says Kay. Health-care services, proximity to grocery stores, pharmacies and your doctors' offices, and making sure your home is safe for later years are most important. You will also likely start spending more on your health needs.

The no-go years: In this last stage of retirement, says Kay, you depend largely on someone else—or lots of people—to help you navigate your life. You may need basic help with driving or personal care, or you may need more significant assistance.

funds. The idea is to make sure that money earmarked for the future is invested appropriately for the time horizon you expect to need it—say, 20 years or so. "You may be a little uncomfortable with a level of risk, but you need the return," says Kay. "It's all a trade-off so that at the end of the day, [you have] the security of knowing you won't run out of money."

10. Hold off on Social Security. The longer you wait to collect, the more money you'll get every month. Your monthly payments go up by about 7 percent for each year you delay—so even though you can start drawing Social Security at age 62, waiting until age 67 makes a big difference. A bigger check means more monthly income from one source—and less from your investments. And Social Security benefits also increase for cost of living—if you start at a higher rate, that cost-of-living increase, even if meager some years, starts out on a higher base, so you're always ahead.

11. Consider long-term-care insurance. Long-term care is expensive even for the basics: Care in a facility can cost thousands of dollars per month, and home visits by a nurse can run upward of $100 per hour and about half that for less-skilled personal assistance. Kay recommends people who need the insurance—that is, all but the very rich or those with very few assets or savings—buy it sometime in their 50s or early 60s at the latest.

12. Don't let a lawsuit ruin your retirement. Seniors may be more vulnerable to lawsuits, so consider increasing your liability insurance coverage as you age. Ask your agent about an "umbrella policy" if you don't have one, suggests investment firm T. Rowe Price. Most wealthier seniors carry extensive umbrella policies,

> **$ TOP SECRET!** In early 2013, 57 percent of all U.S. workers had less than $25,000 in total household savings and investments—not including their homes—according to an Employee Benefit Research Institute survey. And only 28 percent thought they had enough to retire comfortably.

which cover all sorts of liabilities, be it a car accident or anything else you could be liable for. What you don't want: the assets in your bank and investment accounts or your home being tapped to pay a lawsuit because you don't have enough insurance.

13. Yes, you really DO need a will and an estate plan. An estate plan is not exactly the same as a will, but it's probably just as important— even if you only have a few investment accounts and a house and its contents, you need a plan, says Irvine, California-based independent financial adviser Louis Barajas. Why? Well, imagine you got really ill tomorrow and couldn't explain your wishes. Or what if you died tomorrow without a plan? Would your children argue over your wishes, or would they wonder why you didn't ever make them clear? An estate plan covers all those bases. A will, of course, is a necessity to make sure you are able to pass along your assets—money and otherwise—easily. If you do not have a will when you die, your property and assets will generally pass according to the state's laws. That means your plans to give $10,000 to charity are pretty unlikely to happen since the money is more likely to pass to your spouse or kids.

13 Things Rich People Won't Tell You about Having Fun in Retirement without Spending a Fortune

1. Retire later. Some 70 percent of wealthy wage earners say they don't plan to retire until they're in their 70s, if at all. That's not a bad concept. The line between work and retirement in recent years has been blurring for all sorts of reasons, both economic and personal, according to Fidelity Investments, one of the largest servicers of 401(k) retirement plans. Some people need to work longer; others want to. But regardless of the motivation, "delaying retirement by working just a few years longer can potentially increase retirement income more than any other single step," according to Fidelity. In some cases, delaying retirement just two or three years can increase monthly retirement income by hundreds of dollars per month.

2. Only MOSTLY retire. The wealthy don't plan to stop working even after retirement: Some 60 percent of people with more than $1.5 million saved said they expected to work in one form or another for as long as possible, according to a Barclay's Wealth survey, citing unpredictable retirement costs, return on investments, and taxes. It's worth considering: Even the smartest budgeters still have Christmas gifts to buy, an extra visit to see the grandkids, or a dream trip that they didn't plan for. Consider working seasonally or part-time, as little as 10 to 12 hours per week, to pad your checking account both for those extras you really look forward to and for the unexpected. Just be careful about how much you earn—too big a paycheck each year risks having your Social Security benefits trimmed.

3. Stay sharp. As an added bonus, working even a little in retirement can keep your mind sharp. Michael Kay, the New Jersey financial adviser, says he has a client who was a former executive. He's been retired for four or five years and doesn't need the money that part-time work brings in. But even so, he takes on occasional paid consulting gigs. "It keeps him in something he's interested in and keeps him mentally active," Kay says.

4. Mine your experience. You've learned a lot in life, and those skills are priceless to many nonprofit and charitable organizations. Think about what causes and activities you find most rewarding and fulfilling, then do some research to find local groups that match up and where you can make a difference. Where to start? Try Serve. gov, VolunteerMatch.org, and HandsOnNetwork.org, which use interests, keywords, and locations to find volunteer opportunities.

5. Take advantage of all your age offers—in discounts. You won't be anywhere near retirement age when that AARP card comes in the mail.

💰 TOP SECRET! Living in a high-tax state can take a big bite out of your retirement income—California, Rhode Island, Vermont, Connecticut and Nebraska all have high taxes, including taxes on pension income; all except California tax some or all Social Security benefits. There's a reason so many wealthy Northeasterners spend just over half the year in Florida: They can claim it as their state of residence and pay no income tax—rather than upwards of 6.5 percent in, say, Connecticut.

But you will love those discounts. Aging does have its benefits, and one of them is senior discounts. Lower prices at restaurants; special shopping days at the craft store; discounts on hotels; travel, train tickets, and more. Take advantage—a few dollars here and there can add up to a few hundred dollars a month, even if it means eating at your favorite restaurant on Wednesdays for the senior 2-for-1 dinner or shopping at the grocery store on Tuesday afternoons to snag a 10 percent discount for those over 60.

6. Surround yourself with "miser advisers." Jeff Yeager, author of *How to Retire the Cheapskate Way,*

> **💰 TOP SECRET!** Elderhostel includes a learning component in its travel programs, which are created in collaboration with educational institutions, museums, parks, and other facilities. It offers some in North America for about $600, excluding transportation, as well as need-based scholarships that can cut a traveler's cost to $100.

attributes his spending savvy to a network of some 3,000 "miser advisers," he told Marketwatch.com. They provide him with real-life examples of unusual ways to earn income in retirement and spend smartly by prioritizing what they want to spend on and trimming everything else. You can find your own network of miser advisers. Find other retirees or pre-retirees with the same penchant for a rich retirement that doesn't cost a fortune, and share tips and advice.

7. Trim around the edges to spend bigger on the fun stuff. Can you cut cable? Relieve the lawn guy of his duties? Keep the thermostat up or down a few degrees? Cut back on eating dinner out except, say, once a week? Barb, a widow, early retiree, and blogger in Texas, writes that she's trimmed her expenses in small ways, including going to matinee movies, borrowing books from the library, and reevaluating her cell phone and insurance plans. Some only save a few dollars a month, others a bit more. But the little things have made a big difference, Barb writes, leaving more money for things she really enjoys.

8. Consider going abroad—to live. It might seem like a pipe dream, but the lower cost of living in many foreign countries can actually lead to a fabulous, rich-guy quality of life—even including the cost of traveling back to the States for family visits. Consider places like Belize, Argentina, Costa Rica, Panama, or even Thailand, where Americans can often retire on less than $1,500 a month for a luxury lifestyle. On the coast of Ecuador, you could rent an apartment for $400 a month or buy a condo for about $40,000. Restaurants serve prix-fixe lunches for under $3, and fruits and vegetables cost pennies on the dollar compared to U.S. prices. But if you decide to pursue the option, consider the costs of taxes and the level of health care you can access. Check out sites like Expatistan.com, which has a cost-of-living calculator for cities worldwide; VisaHQ.com, a resource for all types of visas and related information; and InternationalLiving.com, which has a section dedicated to retiring abroad.

9. Travel on your time—and avoid everyone else's.
Just like that rich-guy vision gives you the foresight to travel in shoulder season for big savings, traveling smart in retirement can net big savings. Working people travel weekend to weekend and often pay higher Friday and Sunday airfare. You, on the other hand, can travel on Tuesdays and come back on Saturdays to snag hotel bargains and midweek specials that are only available on, say, Wednesdays. You can also travel during the least busy times without worrying about a school schedule or getting back to the office. The savings, say experts, can be upward of 50 percent on a five-day trip.

Become an Instant Expert
3 Little-Known Facts about Social Security

1. Just about anybody who has worked for 10 or more years is eligible for Social Security retirement benefits. To qualify, you need 40 quarters of employment and to have earned a minimum income per quarter. The amount of earnings goes up a bit each year; it was $1,160 for 2013. You could fulfill that with seasonal and temporary work in the summer or winter.

2. If one partner in a marriage earns significantly less than the other, the lower-earning spouse can collect spousal benefits rather than payouts based on his or her own earnings history. The person who made less can take either the benefits that he or she earned or wait until their spouse starts receiving benefits and collect 50 percent of that amount. A divorced spouse who was married for more than 10 years and hasn't remarried can draw against their ex's work history. Widows and widowers can receive the higher of their own or their spouse's monthly payment, but not both.

3. For most people, Social Security is one component of retirement income—one leg of the so-called three-legged stool. Pensions are another component, but these days few workers get a pension. The last leg is personal savings, whether in a 401(k) plan, IRA, investment account, or savings account.

10. Find a retirement-friendly income tax state to live in. In retirement, minimizing taxes is a matter of degrees. Several states have no tax on income: Alaska, Florida, Nevada, South Dakota, Texas, Washington, and Wyoming. New Hampshire and Tennessee only tax dividend and interest income—a big source of income for retirees living off their investments. There are nine states that exempt all federal, military, in-state pensions, and Social Security benefits from income tax:

Alabama, Hawaii, Illinois, Louisiana, Massachusetts, Michigan, Mississippi, New York, and Pennsylvania; Alabama, Hawaii, and Illinois also do the same for some private pensions. Pennsylvania and Mississippi are unique in that they are the only states that exempt all retirement income—even IRA and 401(k) distributions.

11. Don't forget about property taxes when choosing a place to retire. Property taxes pay for services and schools. And they almost always go up. In high-tax communities, some property-tax rates have doubled or tripled over the last decade. All states offer some level of exemption for homeowners, and often more for seniors, and some states also offer seniors additional school-tax relief. The Tax Foundation in Washington, D.C., found that residents of Louisiana, Hawaii, Alabama, the District of Columbia, Delaware, and Mississippi paid the lowest property taxes compared to the value of their homes. Florida came in at the middle of the pack.

12. Give up status symbols and big-ticket items from pre-retirement life. Bankrate.com profiled couples who retired early but still live well without a fortune. Among them: Gary, who retired at 49, and his wife, Julie. They cut their expenses since they live on about half of their pre-retirement income. The biggest savings and one that makes their life in the U.S. Virgin Islands affordable: They gave up status items, the couple told Bankrate.com. They sold their two Mercedes-Benzes, ditched their designer-label buying habit, and abandoned what they described as a "country club lifestyle." They live more simply but still have plenty of fun in their island life.

13. Travel your age. Most hotel chains have senior discount programs—including a loyalty program that cuts 50 percent off of room rates at Starwood Hotels (including Sheraton, Four Points, W Hotels, and Westin Hotels and Resorts) and a 40 percent discount from the Hilton Senior Travel Honors Program. The Starwood program is free; the Hilton program comes with a $55-per-year membership fee. Elderhostel, now known as Road Scholar, offers nearly 8,000 travel programs worldwide and appeals to the adventurous sort among the 55-and-older crowd. You can also consider going with a group—without spending the luxury price.

13 Ways Rich People—and You—Make Their Home Work for Them

1. Refinance 10 to 15 years before retirement. If you're in your 50s and you still have 15 years or more left on your 30-year mortgage, consider refinancing. For one, you likely have more income now than you did when you took the mortgage out. And when rates are low, it's practically free money to borrow for a short-term refinance. Your term may be 5 to 10 years shorter, but with rates at half the prevailing interest rate for a 30-year mortgage, your payments may not go up much at all. The upside: Your home is paid off before you retire.

2. Keep paying your mortgage—to yourself. If you pay off your house before you retire, you can save those dollars to fund your retirement home, contribute to an annuity, pad your retirement accounts, or make small improvements to your home to make it easier to sell

$ TOP SECRET! A survey by Ameriprise Financial in 2013 found that nearly half of working Americans over the age of 50 said they were relying on their homes to help finance their retirement.

or live in during retirement. Freeing up cash that close to retirement can also help ease the burden of, say, paying for college for Junior.

3. Rent back from the bank. If you are already retired and want to stay in your home, a reverse mortgage—in which you borrow money against your home's value—could be an option. A reverse mortgage provides tax-free income that can help manage the costs of retirement. The home stands as the collateral for the loan, and there's no repayment of the mortgage principal or interest until the borrower dies or the home is sold, according to Investopedia.

4. Downsize sooner to cut costs. So your daughter is in college, your son has his first job after graduation, and you're left in a 2,200-square-foot, 4-bedroom home. Just the two of you. Do you need to pay higher taxes for a home you only use half of? Better yet, what could you do with the money you save on heating bills and maintenance? Downsizing your house for a smaller home or townhome in your same hometown lowers your costs—from taxes to heating oil—and the proceeds could add to your retirement accounts.

5. Consider downsizing to an "edge" area. If you're paying sky-high taxes to live in a good school district but the kids have long since graduated, consider moving to those "edge" areas—you know, the edge of town where one street over is in the next town whose taxes are 20 percent lower. Whatever your savings, use them to pay down debts—you don't want to carry those into retirement—or build up your nest egg. Just saving $500 per month for the next 10 years turns in to $6,000 per year and $60,000 over the course of a decade, Investopedia notes, even if you stuff it in your mattress.

6. Sell and annuitize. If you don't need some or all the proceeds from the sale of your house to buy another one, and you want a stable investment, consider buying an annuity, which are primarily used to provide a steady cash flow in your retirement years. Usually you buy an annuity and contribute to it over time; after you retire, it's paid out in steady amounts. But you can also buy an annuity in a lump sum. It can be designed to pay out over a short or long period—for as long as you or your spouse are alive—or even in a lump sum, says Investopedia. You can also dictate a specific period of time—say, 20 years—for payouts to a trust fund or your estate, regardless of how long you or your spouse live.

7. Stay where you are—with some adjustments. Aging in place and universal design are about building or modifying places and spaces—both public and private—to accommodate people of all ages and abilities. An age-friendly home includes wider doorways to accommodate wheelchairs and walkers, accessible controls and switches, and easy-to-use handles. You can contact a certified aging-in-place

√ The **REAL** World

You've spent decades paying off your mortgage, making improvements to your home here and there, and looking to the day when all that equity would help finance the home you'll live in during retirement.

For many, decades spent paying off a home pays off in a different way: The proceeds of a sale can pay for a home to retire in, pad savings, and sometimes provide spending money to fund the extra frills a more limited income might not always leave room for.

Just ask Patricia and Vinny. The New York couple bought their home in a leafy suburb more than 25 years ago for $80,000. While they put about $120,000 worth of improvements into the place—including adding a family room and expanding the kitchen—they paid off their mortgage more than five years ago and kept putting aside the monthly mortgage cost to save for a retirement that they hoped would include a custom-built home in South Carolina. Their New York house is being sold for $525,000—a profit of $325,000—and their southern retirement home is being readied for their arrival in the summer of 2013.

Patricia was a school-district secretary most of her career, and Vinny worked in a trade. Their South Carolina home will cost less than $250,000 to build and furnish, and more than one-third comes directly from the mortgage payments they'd been saving the last five years since paying off their house. After paying for the new house, they plan to use their sale proceeds to supplement Patricia's expected pension and a retirement fund that Vinny will start drawing from in a few months, and to fund at least one or two dream vacations.

specialist via the National Association of Home Builders to help incorporate some of these features in your home. And universal design features are a good long-term investment for the home itself.

8. Move closer to who you want to be with. If you don't already live near family or good friends, consider moving closer so that you can spend time with them rather than spending money on travel and entertainment. Kay says he has had clients who move to their dream retirement locale only to find themselves too far away from family and friends. They end up moving back, sometimes at big expense.

> **$ TOP SECRET!** An AARP survey revealed that more than half of boomers view aging in place as a major long-term-care concern, 49 percent supported the availability of LTC services for aging in place, and 59 percent strongly supported redirecting nursing-home funds toward home- or community-based services instead.

9. Go downtown. Move to an area with good public transportation and a bustling downtown. That allows you to unload one or all of your cars and drop loan or lease fees—as well as fuel, repair, and maintenance costs—from your monthly budget, says the Michigan Association of CPAs. It also makes it easy to stay active in retirement while holding down your costs.

10. Explore alternative living. No, not an alternate lifestyle: There is a growing array of housing options for seniors who may—or may not—want to live the typical in-a-single-family-home sort of life. And of course, at some point in retirement, you may want to move from a house to an apartment, continuing-care complex, or assisted living.

Become an Instant Expert
Five Design Musts for Aging in Place

Aging in place, universal design, age-friendly communities . . . Today's Boomers are quite interested in these buzzwords, especially as they've watched their own parents transition to assisted living or nursing homes that they'd rather not call home. Just how interested are they?

The 78-million-plus Boomers have a powerful voice: Aging in place is now a hot industry, with products, programs, and professionals designed for consumers who want to stay in their own home. Proof positive—Google "aging in place" and you'll get an impressive 105 million hits. It's a dynamic niche, and one that's evolving as quickly as the Boomers and seniors determined to stay home.

Universal design can be a win-win for sandwich generation Boomers caring for aging parents and their children at home, for grandparents raising grandchildren and great-grandchildren, and for all who are facing the challenges of caring for a loved one with Alzheimer's or other chronic diseases. Whether your family needs the support now or down the road, universal design features are a good long-term investment for the home itself. It can cost between $20,000 and $40,000 to turn your home into a place to age gracefully, which may increase its resale value, so it's an investment in your future one way or the other. So what does an

11. Live LIKE a retiree. Planning to retire in 10 or so years? Check out over-55 communities, which are geared toward the retired or about-to-retire set. Some people in these communities still work full-time. There may be organized community activities or events, but the main point of such 55-plus communities is to live among active adults with similar interests and in the same age group. You can find both rental age-friendly home look like? AARP.org outlines the most important elements of universal design:

No-step entry: You should have at least one step-free entrance—either at the front, back, or side of the house--so everyone, including wheelchair users, can enter the home easily and safely.

Wide doorways and hallways: A doorway that is at least 36 inches wide is great when you're bringing home a new mattress or couch, but it's even better when someone you care for, or a regularly visiting friend or family member, is in a wheelchair. Also, hallways that are 42 inches wide are good for multigenerational family members with varying "mobilities."

One-floor living: Access to essential rooms without the use of stairs makes life more convenient and safe for residents ages 0 to 100. You could consider turning a formal dining room or extra den into a bedroom to accommodate. If you're considering adding a bathroom to your first floor, make it handicap accessible.

Easily accessible controls and switches: A person in a wheelchair can reach light switches that are 42 to 48 inches above the floor. Thermostats should be placed no higher than 48 inches off the floor, and electrical outlets 18 to 24 inches off the floor. Keep these measurements in mind when modifying your home.

Easy-to-use handles: Consider replacing twist/turn doorknobs and faucets with lever-style handles for (painless) ease of use.

SOURCE: © 2013 Seniors For Living.

communities and owner-occupied communities in the 55+ arena.

12. Plan for the inevitable—or at least the very likely. Like to have a game plan for the future? You'll appreciate how continuing-care facilities can adapt as you age, regardless of how your health or mobility changes. Continuing-care communities offer everything from basic assistance with daily living to specialized nursing care. Expect to pay about $1,500 to $5,500 per month, depending on the amenities, plus entrance fees that can reach $150,000 or more. In some cases, some of those fees are refundable to relatives after you die. Most people use the proceeds of selling their home to pay the entry fee. The average age of continuing-care residents at entry is about 80 years old.

13. Just because the bank will give you a home-equity loan doesn't mean you should take it. Borrowing from your home's equity can be complicated—and expensive—for retirees, since real estate isn't liquid and you have few ways to increase your income to pay back the loan. Don't take a home-equity loan to finance your day-to-day living expenses. If you need to make a big repair or, say, find money to renovate so you can retire in place, a home-equity loan can be a decent option, but only if you have the extra cash or can easily pick up part-time work to earn it and repay the loan without hurting your finances.

Great Advice
Where and How Should I Live?

. . . .

Here's a snapshot of three senior housing choices to consider along the way for yourself or for an aging parent facing a where-next decision.

Assisted living: Seniors who can remain independent but need some help with basic activities (like taking care of the home, laundry, meal preparation, and some simple health maintenance) find assisted living to be a great fit. Residents often describe a community atmosphere as opposed to an "institutional" feel. Monthly costs may range from $1,800 to $3,000. Medical care, however, is not included in most assisted-living communities, so keep that in mind.

Assisted living isn't intended to be a permanent place to live. When residents get sick or too old to take basic care of themselves, many facilities will insist they leave, and state law often requires that they do. In Florida, for example, an assisted-living facility with a basic license isn't allowed to tend to a resident who is bedridden for more than seven days in a row.

Independent living: Active seniors who want to live out their golden years without the stress or strain of managing their home find independent-living communities to be like one long vacation. Also called retirement communities, these residences are private, but the option to take part in group activities—plus parties, sports, book clubs, and more—is always there. Costs of independent communities can range from $1,300 to $3,500 per month for rentals, including association fees. You can buy in many of these communities, too. And the fees go toward maintenance and some activities sponsored by the homeowner's association.

In many cases, clubhouses or social clubs will be offered, but it's not unusual for an independent-living community to offer no group-oriented services at all. So do your homework and consider what kind of place you want to live—something more social and group-oriented, or with amenities and people like you without the forced social aspect. Most residents are active seniors who are healthy enough to do all of the activities of daily living without assistance. Many residents of such communities still drive, some are employed part-time, and almost all maintain active lifestyles and ties to the community.

Continuing-care communities: Continuing care typically starts with a cross between independent and assisted living—you'll live in a 1- or 2-bedroom apartment in a complex where a housekeeper will tidy up for residents once or twice a week and a manager will check to make sure you're okay each day. You'll likely have a meal plan and take dinner and another meal in a dining room with other seniors living in the complex. There'll be educational programs, card games planned, activities, lectures, and more to take part in. But your health care at this stage will be your responsibility—so you'll keep outside doctors. If your health or mobility declines, you may move to the next level—another complex on the same property. You may still participate in activities, but with more help and more personal attention to your changing needs.

Eventually, you may move to nursing care in the complex, where your health needs shift from outside doctors to those in the community. Such continuing-care communities often also offer hospice centers for end of life.

SOURCE: © 2013 Seniors For Living.

13 Things Rich People Won't Tell You about Long-Term Care Insurance

1. Buy early or pay dearly. People aged 45 to 54 account for just more than 1 in 5 long-term care policies, while those 55 to 64 make up more than half of those buying the coverage, according to a 2010 report from the American Association for Long-Term Care Insurance. But the earlier you lock in a long-term policy, the less it will cost over the long haul, according to Genworth Financial, a major provider of long-term care policies. Even if it seems silly to pay $2,000 or more a year for a policy you might not use for 20 or 30 years, consider this: The average daily cost of a private room in an assisted-living facility is $206 per day, or $75,190 annually, according to Genworth. Paying for a policy for 30 years is still less pricey than a year of long-term care costs.

2. But your rates can—and—will rise. In the past, policyholders could lock in rates for a long period of time, but an anomaly in long-term care insurance has meant drastic price increases—especially for those who buy older—in some policies. The anomaly: Health-care costs keep rising, and fewer people let their policies lapse than insurers thought would do so. That, combined with years of low interest rates—which help insurers earn money off the premiums and helps fund payouts later on—have made providing long-term care insurance unprofitable at worst and break-even at best for insurers. That leads to frequent rate increases.

3.Medicare doesn't pay for many long-term care costs. Many people think that their Medicare health coverage will pay for time they have to spend in pricey nursing facilities. But that's not the case. Medicare provides only limited coverage for long-term care related almost exclusively to recuperating from a sickness or injury, and pays only for skilled nursing care and medically necessary services.

4. Alzheimer's, dementia, and other preexisting conditions are sort of covered. Preexisting conditions must be covered by long-term care insurance policies once they are issued. But some insurance providers have a six-month waiting period before coverage kicks in—during which the insurer can drop you. In general, the insurer can't exclude a preexisting condition that you tell them about once they agree to cover you. The same goes for Alzheimer's and dementia. But take note: If you are already diagnosed with one of these when you try to purchase long-term care insurance, the insurer can, and likely will, decline to insure you. Still, be honest. If you fib and the insurer finds out later, your policy and coverage can be denied or canceled.

5. All policies are not created equal. AARP warns that policies offer many different coverage options. You can't predict what your future long-term-care needs will be, so you don't want to be locked in to one type of coverage alone. Instead, consider a policy with flexible options that, say, may help pay for whatever care you need, whether you are living at home, in an assisted-living facility or nursing home. You might also look to buy a policy that will pay some expenses for adult day care, health and other care coordination, among other services. Some policies will even help pay costs associated with modifying your home to make it easier to live in. And newer policies sometimes cover the cost of having someone come to care for you in your home.

6. Think ahead. Premiums go up, your income may go down, and you may not be able to afford the premiums—and lose the money you've already invested, AARP warns. A rule of thumb: Spend no more than 7 percent of your income on a long-term care policy. That may be too rich for most people, and remember, the earlier you buy, the cheaper the policy. So start early and shop around for policies with an eye toward that longer-horizon higher premium. If you buy at 60, you might only pay a few thousand dollars per year, and maybe less. But the longer you wait, the harder it will be to find good coverage for well under that rule-of-thumb amount.

7. You can cut costs with a limited policy. One way to reduce the cost of a policy, say insurance consultants: Pick a policy that pays for just two or three years of care. Data shows that most stays in care facilities typically don't last more than three years.

8. Even with a gold-plate policy, it may not pay out as much as you think. *The Wall Street Journal* warns: "It might cover a percentage of certain costs or a percentage of 'usual and customary' charges. Even if your coverage is designed to pay a fixed amount—say, $6,000 a month—your insurer could determine that some expenses aren't covered; as a result, you could end up receiving something less than the fixed amount."

9. And you could face some odd eligibility requirements when you do need to tap the plan. Long-term care insurance pays out based on one general criterion: your ability to perform daily living activities, like the ability to eat, bathe, and dress. Some policies don't kick in until a policyholder can't perform five or six functions; others require as few as three inabilities before they'll pay. AARP recommends policies requiring assistance with bathing as a benefit trigger, since it can be one of the first tasks that become impossible to do alone. Other triggers include eating, dressing, using the toilet, walking, and remaining continent.

√ The **REAL** World

Beth, a 42-year-old mother of two girls in New York, bought a policy several years ago from a former employer, at the bargain price of $30 a month for extensive long-term care coverage. She's since moved to another job, but kept the policy, at just $10 more per month. "I will never let it go," Beth says. Even though she is about 10 years younger than when most advisers recommend buying long-term care insurance, were Beth to buy the same policy on the open market, her costs would be almost double.

10. Buy through an employer while you can. Some employers offer group long-term care policies or make individual policies available at discounted group rates, explains the AARP. Many group plans don't include underwriting, which means you may not have to meet medical requirements to qualify, at least initially. In most cases, if you leave the job or the employer stops providing the benefit, you'll be able to either keep the same or a similar policy if you keep up the premiums. Because group policies pool lots of people, there's less risk for the insurer, translating into lower costs for you.

11. Don't forget about future innovations. Look for a plan that covers types of care you haven't even dreamed up yet. That way, if a new type of long-term-care service is developed after you purchase the insurance, it will likely be covered. Ask for this option specifically, even if it costs a few dollars more per month.

12. Mind your exclusions. AARP reports that most states no longer allow insurers to require that you be in the hospital or a nursing facility for a certain number of days before qualifying for benefits. But some states still allow such an exclusion, and you could come up against that minimum-day trigger every time you need care—which could keep you from ever qualifying for a benefit. Coverage exclusions for drug and alcohol abuse, mental disorders, and self-inflicted injuries are common. "Be sure that Alzheimer's disease and other common illnesses, such as heart disease, diabetes, or certain forms of cancer, aren't mentioned as reasons not to pay benefits," recommends AARP.

13. You're more likely to pass the medical examination than you think. Just because you are 10 pounds overweight or have slightly elevated cholesterol doesn't mean that you won't qualify for the insurance. "For most applicants, especially the young ones in their 50s and 60s, underwriting only looks at your most recent medical records from your doctor to see what illnesses you've been diagnosed with and what medications you are on," explains AARP. Then you'll usually be asked to take a cognitive exam by phone. But there's almost never an in-home visit. If you've had cholesterol problems in the past but it's been under control the last several years, you'll likely have few issues.

Great Advice

Why Long-Term Care Is Worth Considering

Long-term care isn't exactly something we really want to think about when it comes to retirement. After all, we'll be traveling, soaking up the sun, and playing a few rounds on the golf course. But at some point we won't be as healthy, and traveling and golf will give way to doctor visits and less ability to get around. Long-term care encompasses a range of services someone needs for an extended period of time because of a chronic illness or disability. It includes medical services, such as nursing-home care or therapies, and personal services, like help with bathing, dressing, getting in and out of bed, taking medicines, or preparing meals. Long-term care can be provided in nursing homes, your home, an adult day care center, or a group living arrangement.

Most financial advisers recommend—if not insist—that clients buy long-term care insurance to help cover a huge chunk of what can be massive long-term care costs. Policies vary from gold-standard policies that cover almost everything to more basic policies that require you to pay for a number of weeks of care—a deductible of sorts—before the insurance payments kick in.

Michael Kay, the Livingston, New Jersey-based financial adviser, notes that you can buy a plan with inflation adjustment—that is, the benefits inch up a little each year with inflation—and get a little less coverage when you're 20 or 30 years away from likely tapping the policy and get more coverage by the time you need it because of those inflation upticks.

13 Things the Rich People Won't Tell You about Planning for the Next Generation

1. Have an estate plan, even if your estate is small.
An estate plan provides instructions on how you want to be cared for if you are ever mentally or physically incapacitated and details exactly how your assets should be distributed when you die. A good estate plan addresses the preservation and growth of your assets both while you are alive and for your heirs after your death. It can also help you establish power of attorney and advanced medical directives. These give you the ability to document and control decisions about who should speak for you, care for you, and manage your finances when you can't.

2. A durable power of attorney is a must. When you need decisions made for you—and at some point you are likely to (remember those no-go retirement years?)—a durable power of attorney is one key way to make sure those decisions are as aligned as possible with the ones you would make. You appoint someone to manage your financial affairs, make health-care decisions, or conduct other business for you when you are unable to do so.

3. Choose only ONE kid. Unless they're on the same page, says Kay, it's not a good idea to name more than one person as power of attorney. And, oh, here's one thing you don't want to do, says financial adviser Louis Barajas: forget to tell the kids about your plans. "Explain to them why you named one kid and not the others," he says. Otherwise, you plant the seeds of resentment.

4. It's not just about the assets you have to give. Financial advisers say its increasingly important for everyone—not just the wealthy—to leave more than just your financial plans and assets behind. The wealthy often spend considerable time planning their legacy—what they want to be known for, be it charity, a certain way of doing business, or just in memorializing the traditions they pass down to their children. Have conversations with your children about the values and traditions you hold dear, about the charitable causes and expectations you have for your own estate going toward those things. "It's about the messages and values you want to pass along," says Barajas.

5. Make sure your adviser and doctors have a family member to contact if they're worried about you. Kay and other advisers say it happens all too often. They make a call to an older client and something just doesn't seem right. The next call? It should be to the relative on the list who can check in on you. "I called one of my clients, a widow who lives in Florida, for a typical check-in and she sounded totally incoherent. My next call was to her daughter," says Kay. Advisers and doctors can't make those calls if you don't tell them who to call.

> **$ TOP SECRET!** A general durable power of attorney would let the person make every decision and carry out acts—like signing documents—that legally could be made or done by you. A limited durable power of attorney covers specific events, like selling property, making investments, or making health-care decisions.

6. The hard conversations aren't really so hard. . . . Almost any financial adviser will tell you that having a chat with your family—or several chats—isn't the hardest part of explaining your wishes and plans for your estate. The hardest part: starting the conversation. "When they are done, there is a tremendous amount of relief," explains Barajas. "It's when you never hold those conversations that nobody trusts the other person's intentions" after you die or your plan is started.

7. Be specific about how you want assets distributed. The most difficult conversation is the one that comes because you've never told the trustee or your heirs about exactly how you want your assets divided. "What people put in a will is almost always 100 percent insufficient," says Barajas, who requires every client meet with the trustee for their estate in the office and explain, in detail, what they want to happen—yes, even down to that yellow vintage candy bowl that all the children and grandchildren love and want to own one day.

8. Let your family in on your plans. Let your kids and other relatives know how you've decided to live out your life, what you want to happen when you get ill, how your estate will generally be divided, and what other choices and direction you've given. It might be hard to explain why you left that candy bowl to Jane instead of Johnny, but better to hear it from you and get over it now than to hear it when you die and wonder why you never said anything.

9. Have an advanced directive for end-of-life care— and make sure you tell people about it. "When you are in the hospital and hooked up to machines, it's really hard to get your point across," explains New Jersey adviser Kay. Make your wishes known with an advanced directive, and make sure anyone who might be near you when you need medical care—family, friends, your power of attorney, your adviser, attorney, and estate trustee—know its details.

10. Don't forget to tell the family where everything is. "Where is the original will, who is the attorney that created the will, what are the names of members of the financial team involved? Where are the documents, the tax returns, the bank accounts, and who knows all these things? These are all questions you need to answer for the kids," says Kay. You don't want your family searching around for these things when they should be focused on your care.

11. Explain your financial musts. When you sit down to set your retirement priorities, you might decide that traveling four times per year is most important, or volunteering your time half the week is most important, or taking classes at the local university . . . Whatever it is, explain it to your children. These might sound like personal preferences, but really, they impact your financial picture and they're important to you. Make sure your family understands what you find most important in your retirement. The family may not agree, but they'll know.

12. You can't avoid conflict from the hospital bed or beyond the grave. It's inevitable that someone will feel hurt or left out, even in the closest of families. The best you can do is to be clear and honest to help set the stage for clear expectations. "When kids do disagree, you don't want to get in legal entanglement; you want to promote the idea that even though there are different points of views, we need to find agreement for the benefit of the parent," says Kay.

13. Don't forget to be clear about how you live and want to live. Talk to your family about your current and future living and driving arrangements, explains an adviser from the investment firm T. Rowe Price. If you're older, tell them how long you plan to live in your current home and what you are considering doing about housing if your situation changes. Don't let yourself feel bullied into a living situation you won't be happy with just because one of your kids thinks it would be better for you.

Who Knew?
Infamous Estate Battles

. . . .

Your estate may not end with seven or more zeros, but you might consider yourself lucky about that "misfortune," considering the lengthy, expensive legal battles some families go through to settle disputes over estates and inheritances. It happens so often, there've been television specials, a blog, and a YouTube video series dedicated to the salacious post-death battles families wage. Here are five of the most famous and interesting:

Leona Helmsley. The billionaire New York City real estate developer and hotelier had a fortune estimated to be between $5 and $8 billion, according to *The New York Times*. Her will left most of that money to charity and gave smaller amounts to some relatives. Oh, and she left $12 million to her 8-year-old dog, Trouble, but nothing for two of her grandchildren. In her will, Helmsley said that she had "not made any provisions in this Will for my grandson Craig Panzirer or my granddaughter Meegan Panzirer for reasons which are known to them." The grandchildren contested the will, and in 2008 a judge reduced Trouble's $12 million award to $2 million. The difference was given to charity, and the two grandchildren got a total of $6 million from Helmsley's estate.

Jay Pritzker. He built a $15 billion fortune partly through his Hyatt hotel chain, which he started in 1957. When he died in 1999, the remaining Pritzkers were supposed to run the company together. But just three years later, two of Jay's grandchildren filed a lawsuit against their father, Robert Pritzker, and other relatives, claiming that some $1 billion had been taken from their trust funds. In 2005 the two settled the lawsuit, receiving $500 million each, according to the *Chicago Tribune*. After the lawsuit ended, the family's remaining assets were divided among the other 11 Pritzker relatives.

James Brown. "The Godfather of Soul" was 73 when he died in 2006 and left an estate worth about $100 million. His will was clear: He wanted his money to be divided between a trust for the education of his grandchildren and a trust dedicated to educating poor children in Georgia and South Carolina. According to the *New York Post*, Brown's will even said that if he failed to provide for any relatives, "such failure is intentional and not occasioned by accident or mistake." But Brown's wife and children challenged the will in 2009 and were later awarded half his fortune by a judge.

J. Howard Marshall II. The oil tycoon famous for marrying Anna Nicole Smith when he was nearly 90 and she was in her 20s amassed a fortune of about $1.6 billion. They were married for 14 months when Marshall died. Anna Nicole was left out of the tycoon's will, which left most of his fortune to his son. But Smith claimed that Marshall had promised that he would leave her half of his fortune and the son had prevented him from doing so. The ensuing legal case went before the U.S. Supreme Court twice, but Smith didn't live to see the outcome. She died in 2007 before the case—and others around the disputed estate—was ultimately decided in her favor.

Michael Jackson. The Jackson Five. The King of Pop. Neverland Ranch. "Beat It." "Thriller." All iconic Michael Jackson. His death in 2009 plunged his estate—estimated to be worth $2 billion—into a family battle. Jackson's will said his assets were to be distributed to his trust and from there to his mother, his children, and charity. First his father went to court to claim a share of the estate—and lost. Several siblings have questioned the validity of the will, saying that Jackson was in New York when he supposedly signed his will in Los Angeles. They contended the will was a fake. Meanwhile, as of early 2013, none of the money amassed in the trust—about $600 million—had been dispersed to his three children (the children do receive an allowance).

Great Advice

Talking to Mom and Dad about Finances

. . . .

Before you get to enjoy your own golden years, you may need to broach the tough topic of talking about the future with your own aging parents—from their money matters to where they'll live as they age. Some smart advice from Readers Digest on just exactly how to do that:

Take the first step. It can be heartbreaking to watch your parents as they struggle to maintain the home they love, keep up with doctor visits, budget for expensive medications, and simply try to take care of each other. You know they need support—and they probably know it, too, though they may not be willing to admit it—so how do you know when it's time to voice your concerns? There are no easy answers, but the first step is initiating the conversation.

Be prepared for an uphill battle. If a parent has become forgetful, if you notice your mother's memory slipping or that your father repeats the same things over and over again, it can be frustrating to know that whatever you discuss with them may go unheard or forgotten. Even if your parents are fully cognizant of their surroundings and situation, they may avoid a discussion about needing care.

This is normal. Put yourself in their shoes. They've managed their own lives for decades. It is breaking their hearts to be limited, to not do what they've always done, to have their bodies fail on them when their minds are active and strong. They don't want to be a burden and they simply want to hang on to their capabilities.

Be prepared for your parents to interpret your concern as an attack on their independence, no matter what approach you take. This is why the conversation must happen in person—not over the phone, and certainly not via e-mail. This is a discussion that may literally require handholding, and you need to see your parents' reactions as much as they need to read your body language and feel your genuine concern.

Be respectful. Remember when you were young and someone would talk down to you? Or when no one listened to your opinion because you were, well, just a child? That kind of treatment doesn't feel good—no matter what age a person is. While some older adults may need to be handled with kid gloves when it comes to talking about the kind of care they now require, there is one constant: Everyone wants to be heard and treated with respect.

Plan your conversation before you begin it so that you can avoid making your parents feel patronized or criticized. Approach your parents gently, respectfully, and ask them questions that will not make them feel bad or guilty about their declining health and abilities. Ask your parents how you can help; don't merely tell them, "You need help." Ask your parents what their ideal outcome looks like, then do your best to find a match for their wishes, be it home care, a retirement community, or assisted-living facility.

Appendix

Guide to online resources, tools, tips, and additional information

CHAPTER 1: JOINING THE MILLIONAIRES CLUB

Understanding mutual funds:
  Investor.gov/investing-basics
Online investment dictionary and encyclopedia:
  Investopedia.com
Fee-only financial advisers:
  NAPFA.org
  GarrettPlanningNetwork.com
Certified financial planners:
  CFP.net
Companies' annual reports:
  SEC.gov
  EDGAR.com
Brokers and advisers:
  AdviceIQ.com
  BrokerCheck.com
Brokerage information/banking:
  CreditUnion.coop
  MyCreditUnion.gov
  Schwabbank.com
  TDbank.com

CHAPTER 2: BECOME A BUDGET MAVEN

Spending and saving:
  Mint.com
  Mvelopes.com
  Timebanks.org
More *Reader's Digest* tips for managing your money:
  RDAsia.com/How-To-Manage-Your-Money
More *Reader's Digest* tips for saving on groceries:
  ReadersDigest.ca/
    Saving-Money-Groceries/7-Money-
    Saving-Tricks-Never-Work
  RD.com/Slideshows/Good-Habits-You-
    Need-To-Save-At-The-Supermarket
More *Reader's Digest* tips for saving at the gas station:
  RD.com/Advice/Saving-Money/Should-
    You-Open-A-Gas-Station-Credit-Card
  RD.com/Advice/Saving-Money/6-Easy-
    Ways-To-Save-Money-On-Gas
More *Reader's Digest* tips for saving on utilities:
  RD.com/Slideshows/Easy-Tricks-To-Cut-
    Your-Energy-Bill
  RD.com/Slideshows/13-Secrets-To-Stop-
    Wasting-Cash-Now

Credit card tools:
Bankrate.com/credit-cards.aspx
CardRatings.com
LowCards.com
CardHub.com
BillShrink.com
Paycheck & withholdings calculators:
Bankrate.com
PaycheckCity.com
IRS.gov/app/WithholdingCalculator

CHAPTER 3: YOUR HOUSE AND HOME
Real estate tools:
Zillow.com
Realtor.com
Trulia.com
Redfin.com
More *Reader's Digest* tips on home decorating and renovations:
RD.com/Home/Decorating/17-Ways-To-Decorate-On-A-Dime
RD.com/Home/Decorating/5-Cheap-And-Simple-Bedroom-Decorating-Ideas
RD.com/Home/Decorating/6-Tips-For-Buying-Furniture-Online
RD.com/Home/Improvement/3-Hot-Home-Renovations
RD.com/Home/Improvement/A-Simple-Home-Remodeling-Checklist
Mortgage tools:
MortgageCalculator.org/
Bankrate.com/Calculators/Mortgages/Mortgage-Calculator.aspx
Bankrate.com/Calculators/Mortgages/New-House-Calculator.aspx

CHAPTER 4: THE FINANCIAL ROAD TO HIGHER EDUCATION
Finding colleges:
TheCollegeSolution.com
WSJ.com/Public/Page/Rankings-Career-College-Majors.html
Bigfuture.CollegeBoard.org/College-Search
Grants and scholarships:
FinAid.org
FastWeb.com
ScholarshipAmerica.org
CollegeBoard.com
CollegeNet.com
Scholarships.com
ScholarshipMonkey.com
GoArmy.com/ROTC
College savings options:
CollegeSavings.org
Privatecollege529.com
Odesk.com
Guru.com
UPromise.com

CHAPTER 5: LIVING RICH WITHOUT GOING BROKE
Shopping savings strategies:
HowToShopForFree.net
Stretcher.com
RD.com/Advice/Saving-Money/Deals-And-Bargains-On-Travel-Health-And-Technology
Discounts, coupons and rebates:
Ebates.com
RetailMeNot.com
MrRebates.com

256

Discounted shopping:
Gilt.com
RueLaLa.com
ShopItToMe.com
Fab.com

Luxury on loan:
BagBorrowSteal.com
RentTheRunway.com
LendingLuxury.com

Local daily deals:
LivingSocial.com
Groupon.com

Car shopping:
Edmunds.com
KBB.com
Cars.com
Carmax.com

More *Reader's Digest* tips on car shopping:
RD.com/Slideshows/13-Plus-Things-Your-
Car-Dealer-Wont-Tell-You
RD.com/Advice/Saving-Money/
Best-Deals-And-Bargains-On-Gas-
Cars-And-More

Travel discounts:
Jetsetter.com
SniqueAway.com
TripAlertz.com
TabletHotels.com
Vacationist.com.
ITASoftware.com

Home swapping:
HomeExchange.com
HomeLink.org
Domuswap.com
VRBO.com

More *Reader's Digest* tips on travel:
RD.com/Advice/Saving-Money/
How-To-Get-First-Class-Treatment-
When-Youre-Traveling-Coach

Dining:
OpenTable.com
Savored.com
BlackboardEats.com
ScoutMob.com
KidsEatFor.com
Restaurant.com

Free long-distance video calls:
Skype.com

CHAPTER 6: RETIRE SMART

Discounts:
AARP.org
RetiredBrains.com/
Discounts+For+Seniors/
SeniorDiscounts.com/
GiftCardGranny.com/Blog/Senior-
Discounts/
Sciddy.com/Index.php

Long-term care insurance:
AARP.org/relationships/caregiving-
resource-center
RD.com/Health/Healthcare/Shopping-
For-Long-Term-Care/

Housing:
RD.com/Advice/Senior-Living-From-55-
Apartments-To-Retirement-Housing/

Financial Calculators and Tools:
Bankrate.com/Calculators/Index-Of-
Retirement-Calculators.aspx
AARP.org/Work/Retirement-Planning/
Retirement_Calculator/
AARP.org/Work/Social-Security/Social-
Security-Question-And-Answer-Tool/
Apps.FINRA.org/Investor_Information/
Calculators/1/RetirementCalc.aspx
Partners.Leadfusion.com/Tools/
MotleyFool/Retire02h/Tool.Fcs

Acknowledgements

Special thanks to the people who helped me research and craft this book, especially Roe D'Angelo, Nicole Walsh, Perri Blumberg, and Luba Chernov.

Without project editor Roe D'Angelo, who helped guide me from outline to editing to final reads, this book would not have been possible. Her steady guidance and willingness to pitch in with ideas and even an interview of her own to round out a chapter were the secret sauce of getting this book done. Fiona Hallowell at Reader's Digest helped polish and fine-tune the text. Both were patient as I missed a few deadlines and made others by the skin of my teeth. Perri Blumberg was indispensable in her work interviewing businesspeople and television personalities for in-depth advice and insight.

Nicole Walsh, my best friend, opened her wide contact list to help find a number of the people whose stories you've read on the pages of this book. Luba Chernov's Facebook group for mothers in my Westchester County, New York, town provided introduction to families—and their friends and families outside the area. Those connections were critical for reaching people whose money smarts make up some of the rich-guy vision outlined in several chapters.

My two children, Cullen and Lila, and husband, Keith Slattery, supported this effort, vacating the house for hours at a time—and even a few weekends—so I could report and write. My in-laws Hank and Loretta Slattery also pitched in to host the children while I worked to finish chapters. Finally, a special thanks to Lauren Young, a personal finance journalist I admire—and who taught me much of what I know about personal finance. Without that knowledge, I could not have completed this book with confidence.

—Jennifer Merritt

Index

Also Available from Reader's Digest

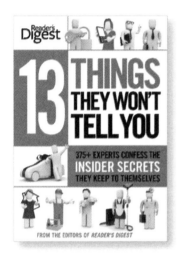

13 Things They Won't Tell You

From the wildly popular *Reader's Digest* column of the same name, this book is a collection of more than 1,000 trade secrets for living smarter, richer, and happier. We asked hundreds of working professionals in dozens of fields: What are the things you wish people knew? What should they know? What do you think people would be shocked to know? You won't believe how many secrets they told us that will save you money and time, get you better service, and help you avoid being scammed.

ISBN 978-1-60652-499-2 • hardcover with jacket
ISBN 978-1-60652-502-9 • Ebook

99¢ Solutions

Walk through a 99 cent store, and you'll find aisles bursting with everything under the sun, from tennis balls and spray starch to rain boots and baby lotion. But everyday items found in these stores can save you a ton of money. Discover simple, inexpensive solutions to common problems, like using hair spray to tame mosquito bites or soaking tired, aching feet in sugarless mouthwash for a quick pick-me-up. *99¢ Solutions* will give you creative ideas for using ordinary items in fresh, new ways.

ISBN 978-1-60652-249-3 • paperback

For more information, visit us at RDTradePublishing.com
Reader's Digest books can be purchased through retail and online bookstores.
In the United States books are distributed by Penguin Group (USA), Inc.
For more information or to order books, call 1-800-788-6262.